Uncertain Path

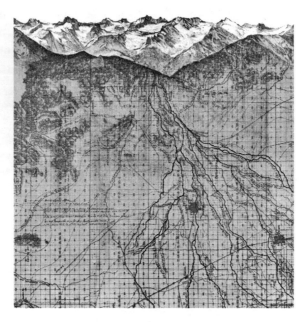

Artwork by Matthew J. Rangel, from his suite of original
prints *a transect—due east*

Uncertain Path

A Search for the Future
of National Parks

William C. Tweed

With a foreword by Jonathan B. Jarvis,
Director, National Park Service

UNIVERSITY OF CALIFORNIA PRESS

Berkeley   Los Angeles   London

University of California Press, one of the most distinguished university presses in the United States, enriches lives around the world by advancing scholarship in the humanities, social sciences, and natural sciences. Its activities are supported by the UC Press Foundation and by philanthropic contributions from individuals and institutions. For more information, visit www.ucpress.edu.

University of California Press
Berkeley and Los Angeles, California

University of California Press, Ltd.
London, England

Library of Congress Cataloging-in-Publication Data

Tweed, William C.
    Uncertain path : a search for the future of national parks / William C.
Tweed ; with a foreword by Jonathan B. Jarvis.
        p.   cm.
    Includes bibliographical references and index.
    ISBN 978-0-520-27138-8 (pbk. : alk. paper)
    1. National parks and reserves—United States—Management.   2. National
parks and reserves—United States—Forecasting.   3. National parks and
reserves—United States—Philosophy.   4. Nature conservation—United
States.   5. Environmental protection—United States.   6. Tweed, William C.—
Travel—California.   7. Wilderness areas—California.   8. Yosemite National
Park (Calif.)—Environmental conditions.   9. Kings Canyon National Park
(Calif.)—Environmental conditions.   10. Sequoia National Park (Calif.)—
Environmental conditions.   I. Title.
    SB482.A4T94   2010
    333.78'30973—dc22   2010005838

19 18 17 16 15 14 13 12 11 10
10 9 8 7 6 5 4 3 2 1

For Frances

CONTENTS

FOREWORD

In the complex world of natural resource preservation, asking the right questions is the first step, and author William Tweed has done this well in the pages that follow. Like the iconic John Muir, Tweed hiked the High Sierra of California and found that the "very stones seem talkative and brotherly." Tweed listened closely. His hearing refined by a lifetime of National Park Service experience as a writer and interpreter, he heard a disturbing undercurrent in the voice of the wilderness. His trek through the forests, and his evenings under an inverted bowl of stars, allowed him to ponder the future of these sacred places and the challenges facing their steward, the National Park Service. Unlike that of Muir, though, Tweed's view was informed by a body of science that indicates all is not as natural or as healthy as it appears. As Aldo Leopold has said, "The penalty of an ecological education is that one lives alone in a world of wounds."

How will the stewards of what the filmmaker Ken Burns so aptly called "America's Best Idea" address the alterations produced by climate change that we are seeing even now? Already we are witnessing increased fire intensity and the lengthening of fire seasons in the great parks of the West. The namesake ice sheets of Glacier National Park are receding and disappearing at a record pace. Rain events at Mount Rainer have shifted from spring to fall and have increased flooding of major entrance roads. Sea-level rise threatens years of restoration work at the Everglades. As climate change is, at least in part, anthropogenic, the paradigm of allowing nature to rule the parks is no longer viable.

Significant challenges threaten our parks, but I remain convinced that the national park idea, the concept that they were set aside for all the people, for the parks' preservation and enjoyment by future generations, is more valuable today than ever. Over the last hundred years of national park management, the definition of "preservation and enjoyment" has evolved. In the early days, we manipulated the parks with a heavy hand, removing predators and suppressing fires. As a result of people like the pioneering scientist George Melendez Wright asking the hard questions, today we are bringing back the gray wolf, and wildfires burn routinely in many parks. These changes in our management have been not only accepted but also embraced by the public, as people flock to Yellowstone to see wolves and calmly prepare their meals in the Kings Canyon campgrounds while a fire burns along the ridge above.

I believe we are on the cusp of another such evolution. Prone to cautious conservation, the National Park Service sometimes lags in response to new science, new ideas, and new paradigms, an attitude that historically has often protected the parks from the whipsawing of political and special interest agendas. Now, as the parks face new challenges, we must again move forward, albeit with great care. If we rush into a new paradigm of manipulative park management based on a new set of human values, rather than those of nature, we risk a competing push from those who contend that, since the parks are already altered, we may as well manipulate them to produce greater economic value. That said, it is time for the agency, aided by scientists and public input, to address the current challenges to its fundamental tenet that the parks must preserve all their resources "unimpaired" forever for the enjoyment of all.

I recently hiked along the rim of the Grand Canyon after a summer monsoon. The smell of desert sage hung in the air, and the low sun backlit misty mesas. The canyon has survived millions of years of change, and its magnificence remains. Now the challenge before us is to see the world with nature and humans intertwined, and to recognize that the survival of all species, including our own, depends on cooperation and collaboration at the ecosystem scale.

Pulling together stories from the past, present, and future, this book speaks to the importance of our national parks and wilderness areas, places that have long served as bully pulpits from which to sound a clarion call for individual and societal action. In a changing world, these unique places remain more valuable than ever. For more than a century, our national park system has helped define our nation, and in the early years of the twenty-first century, that role remains undiminished. I see the national park system as a key leader in meeting the challenges that face all of us in this new century. We must not lose the core values, authenticity, and public trust that have made the parks so special.

Jonathan B. Jarvis
Director, National Park Service

Introduction

This book explores the history, current status, and likely future of the ideas that underlie and define our national parks. In the pages that follow, I outline why the national park idea as we know it, a veritable covenant between national park managers and the American public, is collapsing and will need to be redrawn.

The book came into being as a personal attempt to reconcile what I believe to be a growing contradiction between several intellectual traditions. History, the discipline in which I was trained long ago, teaches the inescapability of change; national parks, the world in which I chose to invest my working life, promise exactly the opposite: that the places and living things we care about can be preserved intact and essentially unchanged forever.

I should note at the onset that the pages that follow focus primarily on only one part of our nation's national park system, a subset I define as "traditional" national parks. By this I mean the grand wild-land parks of the American West, places like Yellowstone, Yosemite, Sequoia, Rocky Mountain, and Mount Rainier. The national park idea as we know it grew out of these landscapes, and to the American public these iconic locales still define the national park dream. To understand these parks, I believe, is to understand both the founding vision and the troubled current state of the national park idea.

Like any mission-based public institution, the agency that manages our national parks, the National Park Service, must cultivate public support if it is to survive and prosper. Public support has always been based on the agency's idealistic mission. Since the service's establishment in 1916, it has promised two things—that the resources of the parks will be preserved "unimpaired for the enjoyment of future generations," and that the parks themselves will be available for public enjoyment.[1] The mission defined by these phrases has evolved in many ways over the succeeding ninety-plus years, but it has changed little over the decades as far as the public is concerned.

Much has been written about the apparent contradiction between preservation and enjoyment in national parks. Despite decades of argument by those who would see the parks more developed as playgrounds, the law reads clearly on this point. Enjoyment must be managed so as to not damage the parks.[2] There is no contradiction here.

Instead, the problem lies within the legal mandate to conserve the parks in a way that leaves them "unimpaired." The agency has wrestled throughout its history with what this means and has more than once redefined its goals in light of scientific discoveries. Deeply embedded in the concept, however, is the promise that things will not change. Many within the agency know that this is not possible, and a close reading of the bureau's *Management Policies 2006* will disclose sections dealing with how to respond to change. But—and this is what counts—the promise to the public has always been that the national parks will be preserved intact, just as the National Park Service Organic Act of 1916 promises.

I know this to be true because I was one of those who regularly made this promise. I worked for the National Park Service for more than thirty years, serving over the years as a park naturalist, historian, public information officer, and park planner. Most of this time was spent at Sequoia and Kings Canyon, the two great national parks of the southern Sierra Nevada of California. Countless times over those decades, I explained to park visitors, park neighbors, writers, reporters, park partners, and anyone else who would listen that the mission of the National Park Service was to preserve the parks "unimpaired for the enjoyment of future generations." Their children and grandchildren, I promised, would be able to enjoy the parks in a condition unchanged from the one enjoyed now. The message, which I often presented as a covenant binding the parks and the American public, almost always found acceptance. Everyone wanted to believe in the national park dream. Not one person ever asked me if the bold promise was actually possible. People should have.

In my last years with the Park Service, I wrestled with the growing disconnect I sensed between the public promise of national parks as islands of stability and what I knew instead to be true. Even as I assured the public that the dream remained intact, I knew change was coming, and that it would come with an intensity and inevitability that would sweep away much that is treasured. This sense of impending change came from multiple sources. Scientists told me that profound biological change had already begun. The very biological assumptions that the parks were based on were no longer true. To make the point even more clearly, other disciplines provided similar messages. Environmental historians challenged long-held beliefs about the origins of the landscapes we treasure. Demographers regularly identified significant and unsettling social changes that threatened political support for the parks. The more evidence I sought about the inevitability of change, the more I found.

I left the National Park Service in 2006. I did so not just because the stories I had so often told no longer always felt true but also because I believed I could do useful work for national parks from the outside. After I left the agency, I set out to search for a new future for national parks. I knew that on such a quest I would also have to consider the concept of designated wilderness, a mid-twentieth-century offshoot of the national park idea. I did this as a friend of national parks, but also as a critic. My quest would be to see if I could make sense of traditional national parks and wilderness in a twenty-first-century context.

I also decided to take a long walk.

ONE

South from Yosemite

Artwork by Matthew J. Rangel, from *a transect—due east*

I may be surrounded by wilderness, but the line of cars in front of me stands nearly as motionless as the scenery. One hundred yards ahead, on the exact crest of the Sierra Nevada, a guide from a large tour bus is negotiating business details with a park ranger who occupies a small wooden toll station in the middle of the highway. The rest of us wait. We ignore the scenery. Instead, we watch the bus, looking for some sign that it has finished its business and is ready to move on into Yosemite National Park. Exhaust fumes from a dozen waiting vehicles mingle with the low morning light. Finally, the guide re-enters the bus, and the door seals shut. With a belch of diesel smoke, the coach lumbers down the highway into the park, its passengers safely protected within its air-conditioned, tinted-window confines. I pull up to the Tioga Pass entrance station. "Welcome to Yosemite National Park," voices the ranger when I show my national park pass. "May I please see some identification?"

A few minutes later, my wife and I are circling in the wilderness permit office parking lot at Tuolumne Meadows, looking for a space. On this mid-August Sunday, vehicles fill every defined slot as well as all the easy places to double-park. On our second circuit of the lot, our luck improves. Another hiker, his business with the permit office completed, pulls out. Like Christmas shoppers, we grab the space before any of the several other circling cars do so. Inside the wilderness permit office, a plywood building with the ambience and layout of a car rental office, we wait our turn. When it comes, I produce my reservation form—this does feel like renting a car—and listen as the young ranger behind the desk explains wilderness to me. I've been hiking in these mountains for forty years, and have issued thousands of these permits myself to eager hikers, but I listen patiently as she speaks. I must keep all my food in a bear canister, she explains, and I will do grievous harm to the environment if I burn used toilet paper rather than hauling it out. I lay out my planned itinerary. She has obviously never heard of my destination far to the south in Sequoia National Park. Her computer does no better. It has no code for the Crescent Meadow Trailhead and prints out my destination as "unspecified." After the form is printed, the ranger adds "Crescent Meadow" by hand. I wait for her to instruct me to initial various parts of the form—I'm still in car rental mode—but all she asks of me is my signature at the bottom of the form. She countersigns, staples an additional rules sheet to the already rule-burdened permit form, and hands it to me. "Have a good hike," she intones mechanically, and then she looks past me. "Next," she says.

I've chosen the parking lot of the Tuolumne Meadows High Sierra Camp as my wilderness portal. Four long rows of cars occupy a hundred yards of asphalt. We spy the John Muir Trail sign in a corner of the lot. Out of the car comes my pack. It's heavy—nearly fifty pounds—but I've spent too many years as a ranger to trust the wilderness. It's an occupational hazard. I think back to numerous official conversations with newspaper reporters in which I explained what had gone wrong with other people's wilderness adventures. Those conversations shadowed me as I prepared my own pack for this trip.

In recent weeks, I've joked with friends that this trip will either make me a good deal younger or significantly older. In the past, I've always been able to count on growing stronger (and younger) on the trail. I'm hoping for the same this time, but doubts remain. I cinch

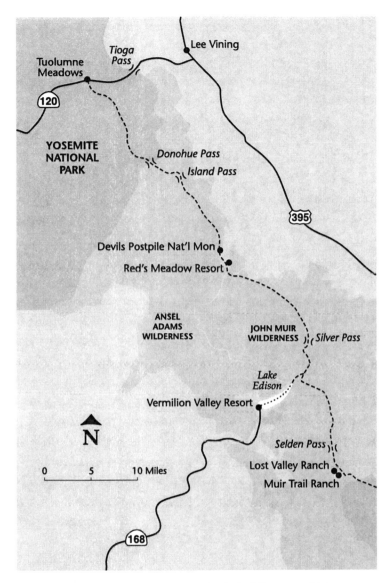

The northern half of the author's hike: the dashed line traces his progress along the John Muir Trail from Tuolumne Meadows, in Yosemite National Park, to Lost Valley Ranch, near the northern gateway to Kings Canyon National Park.

down the pack's shoulder and waist belts and pick up my walking stick. My wife takes my picture by the trail sign, strolls with me for a few hundred yards to the Dana Fork bridge, and we say our goodbyes. I turn onto the John Muir Trail and walk southward.

An important question returns to me within the first mile—what am I doing here? A friend asked me this very question a few days earlier, and, to my surprise, I told him that I intended to make a pilgrimage. Later, I tried to figure out where that had come from. Was I really making a sacred journey? The more I thought about it, the more the idea worked. For many Americans, national parks and wilderness areas are sacred. The ideas that support them possess the power and importance of religion. I am going into the wilderness to reconsider those ideas and seek perspective. In that regard, at least, I am a pilgrim.

I think back to the events that started me down this path. The story started more than four decades ago in my undergraduate college years. I remember the night clearly. Cold rain fell outside the library at the University of the Pacific in California's Great Central Valley. A history student there, I had spent much of that particular evening searching out assigned readings in various historical journals, and now, putting off the inevitable cold, wet walk back to my dormitory, I was simply wandering through the massive maze of stacks that held the collected issues of various periodicals. Now and then, something would look interesting, and I'd pull it off the shelf for a moment of curious browsing. The back issues of the *Sierra Club Bulletin* caught my eye. I knew this title as a modern, slick-paper magazine and didn't recognize the volumes before me, which consisted of a long series of tan-covered paperback books, each running to a hundred pages or more. I pulled one off the shelf. A new world opened.

In the succeeding weeks, spending time in the old *Bulletins* became my nightly dessert, my reward for finishing up whatever I needed to do that evening. It didn't take long to understand the basic dimensions of what I had found. From its founding in the early 1890s until the opening years of the 1960s, the Sierra Club had dedicated one issue of the *Bulletin* each year to a literary summary of things of interest to the club's members. During most of those seventy years, this had meant what was going on in the Sierra Nevada. The stories fascinated me. I read reports of exploring parties in the 1890s; of early outings to Tuolumne Meadows, the Kings Canyon, and the Kern River by surprisingly large groups; and of women in long skirts and hobnail boots climbing summits still ranked as difficult. Names came into focus: John Muir, Theodore Solomons, J. N. Le Conte.

This history captured me because, like so many Californians of my generation, I had already begun to flirt with the Sierra Nevada and the world of outdoor adventure. Between my junior and senior years of high school, as a casual lark, I had talked a friend into joining me in a foot crossing of the southern Sierra. With five-dollar packs from an army surplus store and sleeping bags so thin we could see through their seams, we innocently hiked across the highest mountains in the forty-eight states. Captured by what I had seen, I wrangled a job the following summer hauling visitor luggage around in a wheelbarrow at a lodge in Sequoia National Park's Giant Forest. I discovered that I liked the outdoor, people-oriented work, and for the next few years I returned to Giant Forest each summer. For a seasonal student job, it paid well. The hotel company gave me almost nothing, but a good porter could collect a quarter per suitcase in tips. More important, I enjoyed being in the mountains. Every day off found me exploring a new trail. Eventually I discovered, as did so many other young people in those years, that the mission of protecting and preserving national parks was something I could believe in.

At first, I was content simply to explore this new and exciting landscape, but soon I began to develop a curiosity about it. How, I wondered, had these amazing places come to be explored and preserved? Once I discovered the early issues of the *Sierra Club Bulletin,* my curiosity about the Sierra began to generate answers.

It would take another decade for me to realize it, but I had found the twin poles around which I would construct my adult life—the intellectual discipline of history and the world of national parks and wilderness. The first provided me with a perspective for analyzing and understanding the human world; in the second I discovered a mission and body of knowledge that held my interest. As the years progressed, I found a way to combine the two when I joined the National Park Service, first as a seasonal ranger, then as a historian, and finally as a full-time park ranger whose duties included being both a naturalist and a park historian. Eventually, I would spend twenty-eight years on the permanent staff of Sequoia and Kings Canyon National Parks, working in a variety of fields, including park planning and public affairs. For the final decade of my Park Service career, I served as the chief park naturalist for the two parks, interpreting their complex natural and human history to the public.

Over time, however, the world that I found intellectually so congenial began to fragment. As any historian can tell you, change is inescapable. Yet, I discovered, what the public wanted the National Park Service to do was to prevent change—to keep things the same forever. And as park rangers, we promised them exactly that—a guaranteed island of stability in a world of disorienting change.

Individually, few of us doubt that the twenty-first century will bring profound change to both human society and the natural environment. Yet even as the daily newspapers bring us face-to-face with such issues, we continue to believe that our national parks and wilderness areas will exist as exceptions to these inescapable trends. In my last years with the Park Service, this problem plagued me profoundly. Even as I told the public about the agency's efforts to preserve the parks "unimpaired for the enjoyment of future generations," I knew that the future would not be nearly as simple as I promised.

Now, burdened with a fifty-pound pack and a head full of questions, I am setting out on a personal journey of rediscovery. My primary task in the weeks ahead will be to explore the question of what the twenty-first century's powerful currents of change will mean for national parks and wilderness. I want to investigate what will happen to these special landscapes and ecosystems. Even more important, I need to consider the impact of biological changes on the venerable intellectual concepts that sustain parks and wilderness.

. . .

By early afternoon I've moved into another world. The trail miles slip by easily as I ascend the Lyell Fork of the Tuolumne River. Actually, *ascend* may be too ambitious a word for my progress. In the first half dozen miles, I've hardly gained enough altitude to cross a contour line on the topographic map. As I walk, Lyell Canyon surrounds me with gentle grandeur. Pleistocene-era glaciers rounded and smoothed this canyon to near-perfect proportions. Although the maps call it a canyon, the word is too harsh for this gentle landscape. The Lyell Fork occupies a sunny, open valley surrounded by polished granite. Open meadowland frames the river. Within the confines of this greensward of lush sedge, the Lyell Fork meanders gently. Beyond the meadow's edge, elegant concave slopes rise through thin subalpine forest to barren ridges that still display patches of last winter's snow. I'm walking through a giant Hudson-River-school diorama, a landscape that could easily have been conjured up to meet the aesthetic demands of nineteenth-century painters like Bierstadt, Moran, or Californian William Keith.

I may be in wilderness, but people surround me. Day-hikers, many of them fishing, explore the meadows. Several groups of backpackers pass me, saying hello as they march by. While I lunch in the shade of a lodgepole pine, a group of young people wearing matching safety helmets ride by on horseback followed by a string of mules carrying their baggage. Everyone looks happy and at peace as they pursue their activities under a cloudless Sierra Nevada sky.

Our political system has given this landscape the highest degree of protection our legal structure allows. The graceful sweep of Lyell Canyon falls within both a national park and a designated wilderness. Lyell Canyon achieved national park status in 1890, a full quarter-century before the National Park Service Organic Act of 1916 created the National Park Service. Congress had recognized the importance of Yosemite Valley and the Mariposa Grove of the giant sequoias as early as 1864, when it acted to transfer these two scenic tracts of land to the State of California for use as a public park. In the late 1880s, a group made up mostly of Bay Area residents and led by John Muir initiated a campaign to create a large federal park to surround the two small units of the state reservation. This successful effort called for preservation of the new park's resources "in their natural condition."[1] Two decades later, the act of 1916 raised the bar for the management of Lyell Canyon and the surrounding region by establishing the goal of keeping them "unimpaired for the enjoyment of future generations."

In 1984, nearly a century after President Benjamin Harrison signed the Yosemite National Park Act, President Ronald Reagan enacted the California Wilderness Act. Section 106 of that far-reaching legislation declared that 677,000 acres of Yosemite National Park, including Lyell Canyon, would henceforth be managed as a "designated wilderness." This designation placed Lyell Canyon under the provisions of the Wilderness Act of 1964, a visionary piece of legislation that defined wilderness as "an area where the earth and its community of life are untrammeled by man, where man is a visitor who does not remain."[2]

Around me, I see the results of these legislative initiatives. On this summer afternoon, several hundred people enjoy Lyell Canyon as a national park wilderness. Without doubt this landscape has all the attributes they seek. It has no road, only a narrow trail suitable for walking or passage by horse and mule. Regulations ensure that the trail remains closed to mechanized vehicles of all sorts, even bicycles. As a result, "traffic" in Lyell Canyon—and there is a fair amount—moves quietly, at a pedestrian pace. Aside from the trail and a few directional signs at junctions, the canyon includes within its confines no human-made structures. We left those behind at Tuolumne Meadows, when we turned our backs on that busy place with its accommodations, gas station, market, campground, and ranger station.

Nature appreciation began early here. John Muir, still in his first years in California, visited the ice fields at the head of the canyon in 1871. The following year, seeking to prove that those snowy expanses were indeed part of a glacier, he drove stakes into the ice so that he could measure its suspected downhill movement. When he came back a few weeks later, the stakes had moved; the Lyell Fork of the Tuolumne River did indeed flow from what Muir liked to call a glacial fountain.

In 1881–1882, a mining company constructed a wagon road to Tuolumne Meadows, and the adjoining Lyell Canyon area soon gained a reputation as a rewarding destination for those seeking a High Sierra experience. By the beginning of the twentieth century, the Sierra Club, then a small San Francisco Bay Area mountaineering club, had begun to organize an annual outing for its members. The event rotated among a number of Sierra locations, but repeatedly the annual outing centered on a base camp at Tuolumne Meadows, a location that allowed hundreds to appreciate the exquisite beauty of the Lyell Fork and its headwaters glacier. Muir so treasured Lyell Canyon that he purchased a William Keith painting depicting this quintessential Sierra landscape. Keith's view of Lyell Canyon used the Lyell Fork and its meadowlands to frame a view of Mount Lyell and its glacier. Muir cherished the painting and displayed it in his Martinez home until his death. His heirs still own it today.

In 1915, less than a year after the death of Muir, the Sierra Club successfully lobbied the California Legislature for a memorial to the club's founding president. As specified in the resulting legislation, the "John Muir Trail" would begin in Yosemite Valley, climb to Tuolumne Meadows, then turn south and ascend Lyell Canyon on its way to the Kings River country and Mount Whitney. It would take nearly a quarter century to complete the entire 212-mile route, but the Lyell Canyon section of the Muir Trail opened immediately. Existing trails made the canyon easy to access, and those who loved the Sierra already knew the landscape.

More than ninety years have now passed since the designation of the Muir Trail, and multiple generations have come to count Lyell Canyon as one of the defining High Sierra landscapes. Much more than places like Yosemite Valley and Tuolumne Meadows, it has achieved the ultimate national park goal: it appears not to have changed. A 1915 Sierra Club visitor to Lyell Canyon suddenly transported forward nine decades might be shocked by the skimpy hiking attire of modern women (and men too for that matter) and fascinated by backpackers using superlightweight equipment. But that same time-transported visitor would not only recognize and appreciate the visually unblemished landscape but also understand the motivations that still bring visitors to the canyon.

Places like Lyell Canyon, and the High Sierra as a whole, have played a critical role in defining national parks and designated wilderness as they exist today. Yellowstone holds the distinction of being the first landscape to be designated as a national park, but the next three reservations so titled were all in the Sierra Nevada of California. Sequoia, General Grant (the ancestor of modern Kings Canyon National Park), and Yosemite National Parks all came into being in the autumn of 1890, and their creation marks the transition of the United States from a nation with a single national park to one that possessed a national park *system*.

This same California interest in the Sierra Nevada and the preservation of wildlands in the late nineteenth century not only produced the Sierra Club, established by John Muir and a group of like-minded San Francisco Bay Area friends in 1892, but also prompted three men to define and perfect the modern American national park concept. Franklin Lane, Stephen Mather, and Horace Albright all attended the University of California, and each played a significant role in creating the National Park Service and defining the national park system. Lane, serving as Woodrow Wilson's secretary of the interior, endorsed the idea that the Interior Department should have an agency dedicated to managing the parks, and it was he who recruited Mather, a fellow Californian, to lead the political campaign to create the agency. Another of Lane's California appointees had recruited Albright, a recent Cal graduate who had grown up in Bishop, in the eastern shadow of the Sierra. Lane assigned him to Mather as an assistant. Together, Mather and Albright succeeded in establishing the National Park Service and served as its first two directors. To this day, much National Park Service philosophy and policy dates back to the early twentieth century and these men.

In the middle years of the twentieth century, building on the same roots, the California-based Sierra Club, working closely with the Wilderness Society, played a major role in the campaign to create a national wilderness system. Seven times, beginning in 1949, the club organized wilderness conferences, and these events, which brought wilderness advocates from all over the nation to San Francisco, helped build and sustain the movement that finally gained the passage of the Wilderness Act in 1964.

The Wilderness Act differed significantly from the National Park Service Organic Act of 1916. Between 1916 and 1964, wilderness advocates learned, the legislative injunction to conserve lands "unimpaired" for future generations had led, in fact, to extensive tourist development in many major units of the national park system. Development had begun in Yosemite, for example, decades before the creation of Yosemite National Park in 1890, and it had accelerated under the aegis of the National Park Service. Under the leadership of the Mather-Albright administration and its successors, the National Park Service (NPS) had successfully lobbied Congress for substantial sums that were then used to build extensive roads and visitor infrastructure. At the same time, private concessioners had been encouraged to invest significant sums in commercial facilities. By the 1950s, Yosemite had a modern highway system, huge campgrounds, the Ahwahnee Hotel, and traffic congestion. In the high country, the Park Service was reconstructing the Tioga Road, turning it into a major trans-Sierra thoroughfare.

The concept of federally designated wilderness in national parks came as a reaction to this. Originally imagined by Forest Service officials as a way to manage large tracts of undeveloped national forest lands, the concept also appealed to those who wanted to contain development in national parks. By the early 1960s, this included a significant proportion of the members of groups like the Sierra Club.

As codified in 1964, designated wilderness would be managed to preserve its "natural conditions" in a manner that would leave the land as if it had "been affected primarily by the forces of nature.... The imprint of man's work [would be] substantially unnoticeable." Oft quoted also is the goal that the land be appropriate "for solitude or a primitive and unconfined type of recreation."[3]

Lyell Canyon played a role in all this. If a landscape can serve as a cultural paradigm, this is such a place. Its condition embodies the very essence of what we want national parks and designated wilderness to be. The canyon remains, to most who hike its trails, a truly unchanged landscape, an unpeopled place that preserves the natural beauty that is our national heritage and is protected by the full power of the federal government. It is where we can expect change not to occur.

The reality, of course, is not nearly so simple.

. . .

Named in 1895 for a cavalry sergeant, Donohue Pass stands some two thousand vertical feet above the head of Lyell Canyon, where I camped last night. Since 1904, Sergeant Donohue's pass has marked Yosemite's southeastern boundary. Beyond lies the Ansel Adams Wilderness, an area administered by the Inyo and Sierra National Forests.

At the pass, I enjoy the open sparseness of the storm-swept rock.

To the west the Lyell Glacier, smaller than in Muir's day but still a spectacular feature, shines brightly in the morning sunlight. I make out, immediately to the south, the sharp summits of the Ritter Range, a dark massif containing several of the Sierra's most spectacular individual peaks, including 13,143-foot Mount Ritter. Despite the mid-August date, extensive snow still coats the northern and eastern slopes.

I begin my descent. Tiny alpine wildflowers grace this tundra, and gray-crowned rosy finches flit about. In every way, the Ansel Adams Wilderness welcomes me. I scan the terrain for possible campsites. Although ice-age glaciers left very little soil here, small copses of whitebark pine dot the landscape below 10,500 feet. I wander off the trail into a landscape of polished granite and stunted trees. Given the option, I prefer camping away from the trail. I enjoy the privacy that results and the reduced odds of nighttime visits by camp-raiding bears. I find a decent camp, a small patch of gravel rimmed by ice-polished bedrock. Small, snow-stunted pines offer welcome escape from the intense alpine sunlight, and the view promises nice evening vistas.

An hour later, rejuvenated by a midday break, I set out to explore my immediate neighborhood. From the pass, I'd spied a "short-hair" meadow not far from this camp. It didn't seem to have a stream, so I had discarded it as a possible campsite, but it did look like a handsome place. A few minutes' walking brings me to it. Short-hair sedge, a small bunchgrass-like plant usually no more than three to four inches high, provides sparse vegetative cover for much of the Sierra's thin glacial soils between nine and twelve thousand feet.[4] The plant usually dominates the terrain it colonizes, a pattern that results at first glance in a nearly lawnlike landscape. The seasons make life difficult for the sedge. After being buried beneath the snow for six to eight months each year, it usually has only about four to six weeks in which to come to life, grow new shoots, and set seed before the soil dries out. Once the moisture evaporates, the sedge dries too, and short-hair meadows take on a golden hue well before the summer ends.

Now that I'm in this particular meadow, I note that I misjudged it. A small stream flows near its edge, making it a good campsite. I'm content with the camp I've already established, but—and this is a powerful surprise—everywhere I look I see small flakes of glossy black volcanic glass: obsidian. The Native Americans of California used obsidian extensively to make scrapers, arrowheads, and other sharp implements. Fabricating such materials required care and skill. The standard technique employed a tool, such as a deer antler, to apply pressure to the stone. If applied correctly, this pressure could cause a thin flake of obsidian to separate from the mother stone. Done repeatedly, the technique produced edges of surgical sharpness. Throughout California, discarded obsidian flakes provide clear proof of pre-Euro-American occupation.

For the next half hour, I crisscross the meadow until I rough out the dimensions of this huge lithic scatter. On one axis I find obsidian continuously for almost two hundred yards. In places where the sedge grows thinly and I can see the soil, the density of flakes stuns me. In many spots measuring no more than a single square foot I can make out several dozen bits of shiny volcanic glass. In some places, the ancient debris almost covers the light-colored native soil. I have no way of estimating the overall number of flakes visible, but a number in the millions does not seem unreasonable.

Later, back in camp, I make some tea and think about the site I have just visited. Here, in an area that the Wilderness Act describes as a place "untrammeled by man," and "where man is a visitor who does not remain," I have found clear evidence of intense and prolonged human residence. Judging from the scale of the obsidian scatter, centuries of seasonal occupation does not seem impossible. I cannot ignore the fact that, adding irony, this land now bears the name of Ansel Adams, a photographer of surpassing talent, but one known best for defining the American landscape in a style that usually omitted humanity and all its signs.

I have stumbled upon evidence that brings into focus one of the fundamental intellectual challenges concerning both national parks and wilderness. Inherent in both is the concept that Europeans found in North America a "virgin continent," a land where "nature" ruled supreme and where human beings had never played a significant ecological role. In recent decades, anthropologists, archaeologists, and historians have attacked this idea with vigor, demolishing it within academic circles.[5] Yet despite these studies, the Virgin Continent remains a fundamental public paradigm in the world of parks and wilderness.

The roots of this idea predate by centuries the creation of national parks and wilderness. To understand the Virgin Continent view, we must step back historically at least to the beginnings of European colonization of the New World. As much recent scholarship has demonstrated, North America was far from unpopulated when first encountered by European mariners.[6] Large populations of Native Americans, many of them living in complex societies, occupied the continent. Records of the earliest contacts document their presence, but within a few decades most of these people were gone. Current scholarship suggests that the overall population crash that followed contact reduced native populations by more than 90 percent.

Biology drove these changes. Europeans brought with them to the New World diseases that Native Americans had no ability to withstand. Smallpox and measles played the largest role in this process but were only two in a powerful suite of pathogens that had their origins in Europe, Asia, and Africa. Because the people of those three continents had a long history of war and trade with each other, they also had extensive experience with each other's diseases. Over millennia, and with huge population losses as a part of the process, European populations, along with their Asian and African counterparts, developed the ability to sustain periodic outbreaks of each other's diseases. The native peoples of North America had had no such biological preparation for what was about to happen to them.

Significantly, the colonial tradition that most deeply absorbed the Virgin Continent view came out of the British Isles. In different ways, the Spanish and French colonial approaches to the New World valued the native peoples more than did the British. To the Spaniards, the people they called *indios* were both valuable labor and souls to be converted to Christianity. The French, as they explored the interior of North America, saw the native peoples as useful trading partners. Both traditions lamented the loss of native peoples but were largely powerless to prevent it.

The English, on the other hand, perceived little value in the native populations, and some colonists even considered the rapid near-disappearance of the aboriginal populations to be a gift from God. Within a few decades the story evolved further. The memory of the earlier presence of native peoples faded, and another model grew to fill its place. North America was a true Virgin Continent given by God to English colonists for their occupation and use. Such native peoples as did exist had no significance. Their numbers were not large, and their populations faded inevitably as European civilization advanced. Certainly, these "primitive peoples" had not played any significant role in making the continent's landscapes. Instead, "nature," an expression of God's will, ruled the New World. The role of humankind in this worldview was to "civilize" the landscape and make it humanly productive. Similar views developed on other English colonial frontiers, and it is not accidental that other English-speaking countries, like Canada, Australia, and New Zealand, eventually developed national park systems that strongly resemble the one created by the United States.

By the middle years of the nineteenth century, America's relationship with nature began to evolve in new directions. As the nation urbanized and the frontier faded, key figures like Henry Thoreau and Ralph Waldo Emerson, and later John Burroughs and John Muir, began to articulate the beauty and value of the natural world. What they did not challenge was the colonial concept that "nature" and not other humans had determined how the landscapes of the continent looked and worked.[7] The national park idea eventually came out of this tradition. The role of such places was to preserve the primacy of "nature" as the dominant landscape engine. The National Park Service Organic Act of 1916, which both founded the service and codified the purpose of the national park system, clearly incorporated this premise.[8] Outside academia, the idea has persisted largely unchallenged ever since. The Wilderness Act of 1964, coming out of the same preservationist tradition as the National Park Service Organic Act of 1916, incorporated the same cultural traditions.

Today, national parks and wilderness continue to be defined as places where "nature" remains in charge and where the role of humankind is limited ideally to protecting and sustaining natural processes. That this runs contrary to much of our contemporary understanding of the history of North America almost never comes up.

This afternoon, I've seen strong evidence that this landscape is far from virgin. The people who left uncountable numbers of obsidian flakes here must have done far more than just work stone. Numerous possibilities come to mind. Obviously, they hunted and collected fuel. What else did they do? Looking at the landscape as the last light fades, I realize how little I know about what has gone on here over time. What seems inescapable, however, is that to call this a purely "natural" landscape is to perpetuate a long-disproved myth.

. . .

It may be August, but the new day greets me with frost. As I hit the trail I notice two-inch-high crystals of ice breaking the surface of the mud. My morning's route takes me through the rolling alpine headwaters of Rush Creek, then gently up to Island Pass. Adding pleasure to this already delightful morning, I meet people I know on the trail—a group of University of California administrators headed north toward Tuolumne Meadows on a pack-train-supported hiking trip. I count several of the party as personal friends. Last year we crossed paths at the other end of the Sierra, almost two hundred miles to the south. This loosely formed group, recruited mostly from the university's headquarters staff in Oakland, come into the high country each summer. Their presence perpetuates the long-established connection between the university and the Sierra Nevada. My encounter also reminds me that the community of High Sierra hikers is surprisingly finite.

By midday, I have made my way over Island Pass and begun my descent into the San Joaquin River watershed. I lunch on a rocky knob and take in the spectacular view.

Before me stretches one of the most storied landscapes in the entire range. Every Sierra hiker has heard of Thousand Island Lake and its neighbor Garnet Lake, an equally scenic body of water located two miles to the south. Situated on the northeast slopes of the jagged peaks of the Ritter Range, this landscape has been appreciated and fought over for more than a century. From 1890 until 1904 the area fell within the boundaries of Yosemite National Park, but then mining and grazing interests succeeded in removing this land from the park and reopening it to more intense use. Repeated attempts to return it to national park status have never succeeded, but pressure by recreational users did eventually lead to its designation as a Forest Service "primitive area." In 1964, when Congress passed the Wilderness Act, this land became one of the founding units in the new national wilderness system. Originally called the Minarets Wilderness, the reservation was almost doubled in size and renamed for Ansel Adams in 1984, the year of Adams's death.

Ansel Adams would approve of his namesake wilderness if he were alive today. Over the decades, the famous photographer invested nearly as much time in conservation politics as he did in photography. An active member of the Sierra Club, Adams often used his photos for conservation purposes. This collaboration between art and politics began in the 1930s, when Adams served as a key volunteer in the Sierra Club's campaign to create Kings Canyon National Park. After 1930, many of the *Sierra Club Bulletin* annual editions included Adams's photographs. When the club began to publish a series of books derived from the wilderness conferences that it initiated in 1949, Adams's photos often set the tone for the essays prepared by writers as distinguished as Wallace Stegner, Howard Zahniser, and David Brower.

Although his lifetime body of photographic images includes everything from industrial scenes to a powerful series about internees at the Manzanar War Relocation Center, a concentration camp for Japanese

Americans during the Second World War, Adams's reputation rests today mostly on his wilderness images. Over several decades, but especially during the 1930s and 1940s, Adams created a portfolio of stunning images of the American West and especially of national parks and associated wildlands. These black-and-white photos, composed and printed with powerful artistry, presented to the world what is likely to endure as the perfected visual definition of the Virgin Continent concept. Adams's best-known photos capture grand landscapes at dramatic moments. Clouds and low light both illuminate and obscure. Human beings do not exist.

In the Ansel Adams Wilderness, however, people are everywhere. Thousand Island and Garnet lakes not only attract backpackers and pack-stock users but are also within range for day-hiking. Solitude, it seems, is a rare commodity here. In six hours I meet nearly eighty hikers, most with backpacks, and six pack trains with at least sixty horses and mules between them. One pack string of half a dozen mules is led by a rail-thin teenage wrangler perfectly outfitted in cowboy clothes and sucking on a lollipop.

The whole world seems to be on the trail. I meet three middle-age Brits wearing surprisingly clean clothes for hikers and pleasantly civil in that uniquely English way. Father-and-son duos of several ages grace the trail, along with other multigenerational family units. The grown sons seem proud that their dads still hike. I talk for a few minutes to a couple in their sixties who hope to hike from Yosemite Valley southward to Lake Edison, a journey of nearly ninety miles. They describe the starting climb out of Yosemite Valley as "humbling." Their well-worn Kelty packs, state-of-the-art equipment during the backpacker boom of the 1960s and 1970s, indicate that they have been out here repeatedly over the years. I continue south, encountering still more hikers. I meet several additional father-son groups and, finally, one mother-daughter party. I run across a solo hiker whom I can only conclude is addicted to the Sierra Nevada. I ask him where he's coming from, and he rattles off a half dozen Sierra trips he's taken over the past two months. He's been doing this for twenty-five summers, he says, hiking from one end of the range to the other.

For most of these hikers, wilderness offers a compelling recreational lifestyle, something that brings them back again and again. When the opportunity occurs, I ask a few why they are here. No one admits to searching for an unspoiled bit of a Virgin Continent. Instead, the answers fall predictably into several categories. Wilderness hiking is cheap and healthy; it provides a great physical challenge; and for some, the long quiet days and nights help still the mind.

. . .

Two trail days later, I'm ready for a change. From the moment I rise, my thought is that tonight I'm taking a break from the trail. Between Tuolumne Meadows and Mount Whitney, the John Muir Trail directly touches civilization only once, and tonight I'll reach that point. As it crosses the North Fork of the San Joaquin River, the trail skirts the developments at Devils Postpile National Monument and Red's Meadow, staying just out of sight of the roads and buildings. Tonight I aim to indulge. I've booked a room for the night at the Red's Meadow Resort, a small lodge accessible by paved roadway and shuttle bus from the resort town of Mammoth Lakes. I've survived five days of hiking and four nights of wilderness camping. Now I intend to take a shower, launder my clothes, eat dinner and breakfast in a restaurant, sleep in a bed, and replenish my food supplies from a cache I've sent ahead.

Just before I reach the river, I enter Devils Postpile National Monument, a two-square-mile miniature national park set within a sea of Forest Service wilderness. I can tell that I'm approaching civilization. Just inside the monument, I meet a walker in pressed shorts and a clean shirt strolling with a leashed Doberman. Just having the dog on a trail is against Park Service rules, but before I can give this much thought, I encounter the rest of the family. A woman about the same age as the dog-walking man and a preteen girl come into sight. The girl is sitting in the middle of the dusty trail and looks very unhappy. As I detour around them, I pick up part of the conversation. "It would be better," says the exasperated woman, "if you told us right now that you're not going to walk any farther." It looks to me like the girl is already making herself pretty clear about this, but I have enough sense not to get in the middle of this domestic dispute.

Ten minutes later, I arrive at the monument's small ranger station. Since I left Tuolumne Meadows, I've not seen a ranger or federal employee of any sort, but suddenly I'm in the presence of three young park rangers, all nicely uniformed. In my Park Service days, my office at Sequoia provided technical assistance to the Postpile, so I know some of these folks. We chat for a while. I can't blame these rangers for not being out on the trail; that's not their job. The park rangers here are hired to talk to the hundreds of tourists who come to the monument each day via shuttle bus.

I walk through the monument on my way to the Red's Meadow Resort. The stroll to the volcanic formation that gives this park its name, a bluff of columnar basalt, stretches only a few tenths of a mile. As I walk, I gather more than a few stares. Here, in the midst of hundreds of day visitors, I am the odd man out. My big pack, generally dirty condition, and slow lumbering gait distinguish me from the dozens of day tourists. The crowd looks more suited to a city park than to the High Sierra. I see baby strollers, ice chests, and portable music systems.

I am struck by how culturally diverse these visitors are compared to those I have shared the trail with for the past five days. Until now, I had not realized how much my hike has taken me back into the world of mid-twentieth-century California. I've been walking in a trail community that has been almost completely Anglo. Now I'm in a flow of people that includes Hispanics, Asians, and blacks—modern California, in short. The contrast makes me keenly aware of how closely wilderness remains tied to one segment of society.

When I arrive half an hour later at the Red's Meadow Resort, I find a cluster of small wooden buildings standing among massive red fir trees. Oversized American pickup trucks fill the adjacent parking lot. A shuttle bus is just leaving, heading back to Mammoth Lakes and the world of supermarkets and resort hotels. I've delayed lunch in anticipation of something better than crackers and jerky. I drop my pack by the door of the café, where half a dozen other large packs are already lined up, and study the scene. A small campers' store and the café face each other across a dusty plaza punctuated by several large trees and two pay phones. Cut log rounds provide seating for perhaps two dozen people, mostly hikers and anglers by the look of them. I head into the café.

Later, having consumed a BLT and a milkshake, I check into my simple room a few doors away. In other circumstances, my room at the Red's Meadow Resort might be disappointing—two double beds in a worn setting of plywood walls and cheap asphalt tile flooring, some of it missing. The curtains don't quite fit the windows. But when approached as a wilderness interlude, this room has amazing luxuries—running water, a hot shower, and electric lights.

Twelve hours later, I'm back on the trail. My decades-old topographic map indicates that the country immediately south of Red's Meadow supports extensive forests, but a day in 1992 changed all that. A lightning strike a few miles down the canyon kindled a fire that strong winds intensified like a blacksmith's bellows. Within hours, what under other conditions might have been a small ground fire grew into an inferno of wind-driven flames, rushing up the San Joaquin Canyon toward the Red's Meadow Resort and Devils Postpile National Monument. The fire came within rock-throwing distance of both sites, but a fortunate combination of changing wind patterns and fire-fighting efforts saved the developments at both outposts of civilization. The surrounding forests did not fare as well, and in many areas the fire killed the entire community of trees. What had been a dense forest of red fir and lodgepole pine became a blackened landscape of standing snags in a sea of ash. Now, fourteen years later, the biological landscape has moved on. Not nearly enough time has passed to grow a new forest, but the Rainbow Fire zone nevertheless abounds with life. Tall black snags still dominate the scene, but a dense understory of brush and small trees clothes the landscape. Elderberry, gooseberry, and currents prosper, as do native grasses.

My goal today, established this morning in a moment of ambition, is to cover some substantial mileage. This means I need to focus on making steady progress. Almost immediately, however, I am diverted. Within two hundred yards of regaining the Muir Trail, I stop and pull out my binoculars. The old fire zone teems with birdlife. I hike on in fits and starts, seduced by glimpses of nuthatches, sparrows, robins, goldfinches, and woodpeckers. A northern goshawk glides by. A Forest Service exhibit at Red's Meadow described this area as having "burned so hot that even seeds were destroyed," but I do not find devastation. Instead, this is the most diverse and alive landscape of my hike to date. In two miles I see more birdlife than in the previous thirty-five miles. At the same time, tracks in the trail dust document the presence of deer, coyotes, and numerous smaller mammals.

In my park ranger days, I talked endlessly to the public about fire. Wildfire, I told them, is an essential part of the forest ecosystems of the Sierra Nevada. Fires occurred regularly before we came, and we made a profound error early in the twentieth century when the Forest Service and Park Service initiated an aggressive program of fire suppression. Without the regular, cleansing effects of fire, our Sierra forests become choked with excess fuel. If we are not careful, fires consuming this unnatural accumulated fuel will do grievous harm to our forests. To protect them, we must undertake a program of fuel reduction, a goal that can be accomplished in several ways but is best done, at least in wilderness and national park settings, through a program of carefully managed, low-intensity fire. Implied is the clear message that good fuel management will lead to sustainable forests.

Over the decades, I shared this message thousands of times. Just before I began this hike, however, a scientific study dropped a bombshell. A team of scientists from the University of Arizona's Laboratory of Tree-Ring Research and the Scripps Institution of Oceanography released a study concluding that the fourfold increase in fire acreage in western forests during the past two decades has not been the result of fuel accumulation alone; it has also been driven significantly by anthropogenic climate change.[9] The huge increase in wildland fires in western forests, the report asserted, reflects the influence of longer and hotter summers. A news release issued by the two institutions quoted Dr. Thomas Swetnam, director of the Tree-Ring Laboratory, as saying that the study documents "one of the first big indicators of climate change impacts in the continental United States."

Swetnam's statement carried particular weight with me because I know Tom. I've followed his work with giant sequoias for several decades. The Big Trees of Sequoia National Park, some of them approaching three thousand years of age, have long been a magnet for those studying the climate history of western North America. During the 1980s, Swetnam spent much time at Sequoia and Kings Canyon National Parks collecting data from sequoia snags and stumps. During their long lives, individual sequoias collect and record important information about both climate and fire patterns. Annual tree rings document cycles of drought and help date fire scars preserved within the trees.

Through their tree-ring research, Swetnam and his team added immensely to our understanding of how Sierra forests have evolved over the past several millennia. Indeed, Swetnam was one of the primary sources of the fire story I presented to park visitors. But now, Tom was telling me that his own continuing research was leading him to new conclusions. Something profound was going on.

The news release that announced the results of the study quoted Swetnam as admitting that at first he found these new conclusions unconvincing. He came around, he said, only when the data became inescapably clear. What Swetnam had to face was that a new factor, human-caused climate change, had become the "primary driver" of fire frequency and intensity in most western forests.

I reach the edge of the area cleared by the Rainbow Fire and hike on into unburned forest. For the next several miles I ascend a steady grade through a dense forest of fir and pine. As switchbacks punctuate my progress, I consider the implications of Swetnam's study. The year 1992, I remember, was a dry one in the Sierra, with an early spring. It makes powerful sense to attribute much of the intensity of the Rainbow Fire, which occurred in late summer, to a lengthening summer fire season. Fuels had accumulated in this area as a result of past management, but that alone may not have determined the nature of the resulting fire. If Swetnam is correct, then the Rainbow Fire reflected not just fuel accumulation and weather conditions, but also a changing climate regime reflecting human activities on a global scale.

The larger implications are profound. When I first joined the Park Service, I accepted without question the agency belief that there was a "natural" state of things that could be sustained, and I shared with the public the resulting message that natural processes, if applied properly, lead to natural results. But what if this is no longer true? If the climate of the Sierra is changing, then the predictability of natural processes may no longer be reliable. Processes long perceived as "natural" and predictable could, in fact, produce new and unexpected results.

The premise that natural processes lead to natural results is the keystone on which national park management has been based since the 1970s. NPS policies explicitly state that park ecosystems will be preserved through the protection and perpetuation of natural processes. The Forest Service, although not as clear on this matter, has in fact pursued a similar strategy in its wilderness management program. Environmental groups like the Sierra Club lobby powerfully for reliance on natural processes in the Sierra.

I think back to my own experiences with the natural processes doctrine. In 2001–2003, Sequoia and Kings Canyon National Parks labored to produce a new fire management plan. The draft plan, reflecting NPS thinking, called for heavy reliance on the doctrine of natural processes. The central determinant in deciding where to burn within the parks was a sophisticated computer-based analysis that disclosed how far various landscapes had diverged from the "natural" fire cycle. The resulting map produced fascinating insights into the state of the landscape, but its use as a management tool required faith in the concept that natural processes would continue to produce natural results.

The problem with intellectual paradigms is that, once established, they often become difficult to modify or abandon. When national park and wilderness managers first applied the natural processes approach to natural resources management in the early 1970s, it represented a major step forward. By shifting to a management strategy based on processes, agencies found a way to move away from protecting individual objects or particular sets of resources, such as a specific mix of tree species. The natural processes paradigm offered a more flexible response and allowed managers to accept landscape change as long as the causes seemed "natural." But scientific knowledge has moved on, and what was cutting-edge thought in the 1970s is no longer fully supported by contemporary science.

Compounding this question is increasing uncertainty about what *natural* actually means. If the Sierra Nevada's landscapes and ecosystems have been significantly affected by human activities for thousands of years, then the idea that we can perpetuate a "natural" condition becomes deeply problematic. The questions here are bigger than the available answers. Fuels continue to accumulate in the Sierra's forests. Fires will occur. Prescribed fire still offers the most practical way of limiting fire potential. But if a natural-processes strategy can no longer be relied on, how shall management goals for these lands be defined and pursued? How will we know, for example, if our fires are doing more good than harm?

The answers can only come from the field. Scientific monitoring of fire effects goes on, and from these efforts comes data. Good monitoring collects information not just on fuel reduction but also on such matters as tree mortality, natural regeneration, and invasions by non-native plants. Then the analysis begins. Are the results within what ecologists define as the "historic range of variability?" Do our actions protect or weaken the resources we care about? All this, unfortunately, will take time to determine. In the meantime, the weakening of our established paradigms challenges all those who manage or care about the Sierra's forest ecosystems. In a world that was never "virgin" to begin with, where the climate is warming, where fuels still accumulate, and where the concept of natural processes management can no longer be fully trusted, nothing will be easy.

.   .   .

I sense a change. In the heart of the Ansel Adams Wilderness, places like Thousand Island and Garnet lakes provide immediate destinations for hikers. South of Red's Meadow, the Muir Trail attracts a different clientele—long-distance hikers. As I compare myself to these other through-hikers, several thoughts come into focus. This morning, I am both the oldest and slowest of those headed south. My senior status, however, is only a matter of degree. Although some of the other hikers appear to be in their twenties or thirties, many are in their late forties or fifties. This confirms a pattern I've seen since the hike began. A rough tally suggests that baby boomers constitute upward of half of all the trail travelers I've encountered so far.

I know the history that ties my generation to wilderness, for it has been my story as well. Many of us who came of age in the 1960s or early 1970s connected powerfully with nature and the out-of-doors. We knew we were not the first to enjoy wilderness, but the sudden blossoming of lightweight sleeping bags, miniature cookstoves, and aluminum-frame backpacks changed everything. The combination of new technology and youthful energy created an outlet that led one to adventure and freedom. In the late 1960s, backpacking numbers in the Sierra soared, easily eclipsing all past use. Front-country areas of national parks saw similar increases. The nation responded by creating more national parks and even better outdoor gadgets and equipment. Forty years later, our generation's special bond with wildlands and wilderness endures.

Where are the young people, I wonder? In my youth, Boy Scouts and other youth groups made up a substantial portion of the hiking community. So far on this trip I've met only one scout troop and almost no other teens. Why aren't they here? It is easy to speculate on some of the possible reasons. Society today offers young people an almost infinite variety of entertainments, many of them electronic and indoors. At the same time, most of us live under the shadow of daily fear that has become the hallmark of our culture. My parents let me go hiking in the wilderness with an equally inexperienced friend almost as soon as I earned a driver's license at the age of sixteen. Today that adventure, which I look back on as an intoxicating taste of freedom, would be perceived by most as parental neglect or worse. I haven't met many teens on the trail, and adults have accompanied every one I have encountered. Perhaps the kiss of death for wilderness use by the young is the perception that it is something their parents do, or at least did. Certainly, many find it more exhilarating to explore the fictional world of fast-paced computer games and 24/7 connectivity rather than to wander through the wilderness world of quiet and solitude with their parents.

For the first time on this trip I have an animal visitor in camp during the night. Part of each evening's routine has been to prepare for a possible visit by a camp-raiding black bear. I make sure that all my food and toiletries are securely locked in my bear canister, and I empty out my pack so that a bear will have no reason to rip into it. Often, I stack my aluminum pan and teapot on the pack in the hope that I will hear them fall in the night if something attempts to disturb my equipment. About 3 A.M., I hear my pans roll, and that small sound jolts me awake. Peering out of the tent into the faint starlight I see not a bear but the silhouette of a fleeing coyote. At first light I crawl out to check for damage. My canine visitor had gnawed on the handle of my walking pole and chewed on a roll of toilet paper. Judging from the minimal damage done, neither produced much nutritional value.

Decades ago, when I first began to explore the High Sierra, few bears frequented the region. The high-altitude world offered them little in the way of sustenance. But the great backpacking boom of the 1970s changed all that. Bears, always on the lookout for new food sources, began to visit backpacker camps. Within a few years, hikers found themselves meeting bears all over the high country. In response, a game began that continues to this day. Every night, all over the Sierra, hikers attempt to secure their food from raiding nighttime bears. Many techniques have been tried over the years, and the ever-versatile bears have defeated most of them. At first, hikers hung their food in trees, a trick the bears soon overcame. More elaborate systems of food-hanging developed, as hikers tried using agency-installed metal hanging poles, steel-wire cable-hangs, and procedures like counterbalancing. The bears figured these out as well. Experiments began with portable food storage canisters, and some of these proved effective. Sequoia and Kings Canyon National Parks in the southern Sierra went so far as to install large metal lockers at many popular wilderness campsites. These kept the bears away from human food but led to other problems. The presence of lockers tended to concentrate hikers, with resultant heavy impact on certain campsites, and social problems developed as well. Wilderness rangers found themselves removing stashed garbage from the lockers and even breaking up fistfights between wilderness travelers who could not agree on how to share the containers equitably.

Now, thirty years after the peak of the backpacking boom in the 1970s, black bears have become a part of wilderness life in the Sierra Nevada. Along major trails, where campers are easy to find, bears patrol regularly looking for easy pickings. Wilderness rangers enforce a complex suite of localized food storage rules. Increasingly, canisters are required, but only on an area-by-area basis. Effective canisters weigh about two pounds, and many hikers consider them too heavy. I'm too lazy not to carry one. I prefer to sleep at night.

Near Virginia Lake, I meet the day's major northbound party, a group of sixteen hikers carrying only light daypacks. I inquire and learn they are out for two weeks, making a northbound trip from Florence Lake to Yosemite. A pack train supports them, carrying their baggage. An hour later I meet their pack train. A single packer, smoking as he rides, leads six mules.

Decades of hiking have taught me to recognize the enormous cultural gap that often exists between hikers and pack-stock users in the High Sierra. These two groups display many of the attributes of religious sects. Both subscribe to the god of wilderness, but they worship in different ways. Traditional stock users remind me of Roman

Catholics. They pride themselves on preserving the skills and perspectives of their ancestors; they reflect and value experience and tradition. Hikers, on the other hand, can be thought of as Protestants: they have rejected nearly all tradition and are defining a new and still-evolving set of beliefs. Unlike stock users, hikers endlessly seek the next idea or newest piece of equipment. On the trail the two sects sometimes have trouble exchanging even minimally civil greetings.

The party I meet today does not fall neatly into either of these groups. Traveling with the equipment of backpackers, but letting mules carry the weight, the group occupies a rare middle category. Traditional stock users employ at least one pack mule per person, a ratio that provides about 150 pounds of equipment and supplies per person. Counting riding animals, each traveler thus requires two animals. Today's walking group instead relies on pack support of about 70 pounds per person, not much more than a traditional backpacking load. Instead of two animals per person, the group has a total of only seven to support sixteen people.

I suspect that neither traditional wilderness sect would fully trust this group. Many backpackers would see the mules and write these hikers off as traditionalists, while stock users would scorn them because the hikers are walking and using modern lightweight equipment. Watching the group pass with their light daypacks, my response is jealousy. I may have the freedom of a hiker, but I feel like an overloaded mule.

The next morning I begin the eighteen-hundred-foot climb to Silver Pass. The path, up a gentle and thickly forested canyon, takes its time wandering through thickets of lodgepole pine and past wet meadows. By late morning the trees finally thin, and the country shifts to hard rock. I play trail tag with several other groups of hikers. I catch up with two petite young women who passed me yesterday. We chat for a few minutes. I ask them what attracted them to this particular adventure, and they explain that they are students at the University of California, Santa Cruz, a campus with a long student tradition of outdoor adventures. They hope to make it all the way to Mount Whitney.

As I approach the pass, I overtake a Boy Scout troop. Something about this group catches my attention, and it takes me a minute to grasp that these boys are having a good time. The troop has none of the forced-march aura that surrounds all too many youth groups on the trail. The good humor of the boys shines brightly even while they wait for their elders to catch up. On the final ascent I surprise myself by staying ahead of them. I climb the final twenty-foot-deep snowdrift that guards the pass and scramble onto a rocky promontory to enjoy the view. The boys trickle in a few minutes later and offer to share their lunch supplies. As we munch together on salami, bread, and a choice of cheeses, I learn more about them. The troop comes from Manhattan Beach in Southern California, and the boys do a major Sierra hike each summer. After lunch, they ask me to sit with them by the summit sign while their group picture is taken. I'm honored to be included in this obviously well-run outfit. These boys remind me of the best of the many scout troops I saw on the trail in the 1960s and 1970s. Now, they hike on almost alone as representatives of their youthful generation.

An easy mile of trail south from Silver Pass brings me to a perfect campsite. Silver Lake occupies a large open basin at tree line. I find a spot on a granite knoll near the lake's outlet and settle in. I like this place, with its shimmering lake, open meadows, and surrounding rim of peaks. Small groves of whitebark pine provide just enough shelter to get me out of the sun. I read for a while, then simply wander about, enjoying the light, listening to white-crowned sparrows and yellow-rumped warblers, and absorbing the peace of this place.

I awaken the next morning to beauty and quiet. No other hikers camped within sight last night, and my camp suffered no nocturnal raids from bears or coyotes. Far in the distance I hear the faint murmur of the lake's outlet stream, but otherwise perfect silence reigns. I crawl out of my tent, start my stove, and make tea. The sun paints the surrounding peaks with pink dawn light. I prolong the moment. This place deserves more time than I have for it. I could spend pleasant days getting to know this basin and its moods. Instead, I have another date with civilization—Lake Edison and the Vermilion Valley Resort.

As I move south toward Mono Creek, I give up all the altitude I earned yesterday. The trail descends steeply, making its way down the North Fork to the impressive canyon of Mono Creek. Here I meet the Mono Trail, a trans-Sierra route used by native peoples for millennia and first crossed by Euro-Americans in the 1860s. An hour's walk down Mono Creek brings me to the Muir Trail's Mono Creek crossing, where the southbound Muir Trail begins its climb toward Selden Pass. I will make that climb tomorrow. Abandoning the Muir Trail, I continue two miles down the Mono Trail to the windswept eastern end of Lake Thomas A. Edison, a major Sierra reservoir.

I follow the trail signs pointing the way to the ferry, hoping to avoid five miles of lakeside trail by catching the late-afternoon hikers' lake-shuttle to the Vermilion Valley Resort, located at the other end of the reservoir. The ferry landing consists of a small floating platform firmly cabled to the lake's granite bedrock shores. An American flag has been set in a drill hole in the rock, and the snapping of its wind-whipped cloth augments the considerable din raised by the surf crashing on the rocky shore. A crudely painted sign nailed to a juniper tells me to expect the ferry about 4:45 P.M.

Lake Edison supplies water for hydroelectric power generation, and weeks of hot summer weather and the resulting electrical demand have taken their toll on the reservoir, which has been drawn down about thirty feet below the high-water mark. For as far as I can see, this draw-down zone of wave-polished granite gleams brightly. I find a shady spot out of the wind, take off my boots, and stretch out on the smooth, clean granite to await the ferry. I've arrived early and have time to kill. At first I'm alone, but other hikers eventually join me. By 4:30 a fair crowd has accumulated. Backpackers, day-hikers, and anglers sprawl on the granite above the landing platform. We begin to speculate whether the ferry will be large enough to accommodate us all. I fall into conversation with a backpacker from Britain, who tells me that he first discovered the Sierra Nevada a decade ago while studying at UC Berkeley. He fell in love with the range's open wildness and beauty, and every summer, for more than a decade, he has returned to California just to hike in the High Sierra. He has found nothing else to compare to it on earth.

Finally, on schedule, a white speck appears on the lake. As it approaches it comes into focus as a simple pontoon boat with a shade canopy. It swings around and approaches the floating platform. The crowd, now approaching twenty persons, stirs and moves down to the shoreline. We all make it onto the boat, where we sit in two opposing rows on life-preserver boxes, our backs to the outside rails. A row of standing backpacks runs down the middle of the narrow deck. The ferry's deckhand, a tall, athletic-looking woman in her forties, casts off, and we turn into the wind for our four-mile voyage to the resort. Spray from the whitecaps dampens those who sit near the ferry's square prow. It's cool on the water, and I'm glad that I put on a jacket before I boarded. Thirty minutes later we pull up to the landing at the resort. A floating dock provides access to a wind-sheltered beach.

I glimpse buildings and vehicles among the tall pines above the high-water mark.

The Vermilion Valley Resort bills itself as "the most remote road-accessible resort in California," and the place is hard to get to by any standard. A few weeks before I began my hike, I drove to Lake Edison to drop off a food cache and to take a look at the place. I also reserved a room for the night, assuming that it would be in the resort's rustic four-room motel. Instead, as I discover when I check in, I've been assigned to "Big White," a thirty-foot travel trailer perched on a lakeside bluff overlooking the ferry landing. Within a few minutes I'm settled into my aluminum abode, the contents of my pack exploded across every flat surface in the trailer's compact kitchen and dining area. I toss my clothes in the washing machine behind the resort's combination kitchen, café, and store, and return to scrub myself in my trailer's tiny shower stall. Once clothes and body are clean, I pick up my food cache from the resort's bear-resistant storage building and begin repacking my food canister.

Later, I wander over to the café, tuck myself into a small table against the wall, order a beer, and settle in to watch the human scene. I've been alone a great deal lately, and the change tonight is entertaining. A quick glance around the room tells me I've landed in neutral territory. All the sects that worship outdoor recreation are present and behaving themselves. People who wouldn't usually be caught dead in social proximity to each other occupy adjacent tables.

Through-hikers occupy a slim majority of the tables. We're an easy tribe to recognize, dressed mostly in brightly colored if none-too-clean garments of nylon or other synthetic fabrics. We talk trail as we dine, and most of us are incredibly hungry for something that's not freeze-dried and packed in an aluminum envelope. Vermilion

Valley also has a pack station, and the pack tribe, although not as numerous, holds its ground in the room. An old packer (perhaps he manages the station) sits at another table. He wears the stockman's uniform—cotton from head to toe in the form of Wrangler jeans and a checked, snap-buttoned shirt. His dusty straw hat hangs from a hook on the wall. He must be a regular; he flirts amiably with the waitress.

Other tribes are present as well: fly fishermen in fancy, multi-pocketed vests; off-road-vehicle guys wearing camouflage-patterned outfits (are they getting ready for hunting season?); and even a few tourists in shorts and tank tops. I feel like I've landed in one of those multispecies bars in science fiction stories. Peace reigns, however, and I down a big plate of Mexican food with a chaser of apple pie.

Breakfast at the café clarifies the differences between the tribes. Hikers now dominate the room, all driven by the knowledge that the ferry leaves at 9 A.M. Unfortunately, the morning's waitress, a hope-lessly disorganized and visibly unhappy young woman, fails entirely to meet the needs of her roomful of hungry hikers. (Perhaps she has realized that she's landed in "the most remote road-accessible resort in California"?) Tensions build as the clock advances while little or nothing appears from the kitchen.

An additional worry shadows the room. Most of us will head south today, and the Muir Trail's climb out of the Mono Creek Canyon has a bad reputation. At one table I hear a clear voice announce that fifty-three switchbacks await us. In the first several miles we'll have to climb from seventy-eight hundred feet up to ten thousand feet with heavy packs filled with resupply goodies. The gloom is far from universal, however, and when I strike up a conversation with the folks at the next table (we're all still waiting for our eggs), a woman in that group breaks into tears of joy as she anticipates the Muir Trail in

Kings Canyon National Park. She has waited twenty years, she says, for this adventure.

Breakfast eventually appears. Then the waitress has as much trouble finding our checks as she did providing our breakfasts, but all is suddenly resolved when the deckhand from yesterday's afternoon ferry walks in. She takes a quick look at the situation, goes to work, and the confusion dissolves into order. A few minutes later we file down to the ferry and take our seats. The hour of departure arrives and passes, and twenty minutes later an all-terrain vehicle comes down from the resort and delivers the ferry pilot, a scruffy fellow with long hair and a few missing teeth.

.   .   .

Half an hour later, we're back at the upper landing. The crowd rapidly disperses, and I find myself left behind. Forty years of experience has taught me that the only strategy for big climbs is to gear down and stick to it. In the hare-and-tortoise world of the trail, I have long been a tortoise. Today, I'm also the old guy with the big pack. I switch to my lowest gear and begin the climb. Eventually, I begin to pass some of my companions from the morning ferry. I find them sprawled on rocks and logs. Some hikers overtake me and pass on ahead; but I overtake others, and that feels good. For years I've fought unsuccessfully the urge to compete on the trail. Perhaps the trait is so deeply wired into male brains that it can never completely be extinguished. I realize that, without really trying to, I've kept track of who is ahead of me and whom I've passed. I try to clear my mind of this nonsense.

I pass the nine-thousand-foot contour and trudge on. Ninety minutes later I touch ten thousand feet. I'm on top. The trail levels out, and I wander southward through a thin subalpine forest of lodgepole and western white pine. The big canyon of Bear Creek comes into view. I drift off the trail in search of a private campsite and find a nearly perfect one—a small secluded patch of sand surrounded by acres of clean granite. Lodgepole pines and junipers grow in the joints in the rock, somehow making a living in this almost soilless landscape.

I've never crossed Selden Pass, so the new morning brings the pleasure of fresh country. I enjoy my walk up Bear Creek. All seems right in the world. I ascend this broad, gentle canyon under bright blue skies. Yesterday's big climb left me tired, but still I make good progress. I find the two young women from UC Santa Cruz still in a camp a mile upstream from where I spent the night. They had been on yesterday's ferry but took off fast once the boat landed, and stayed ahead of me all day. Now they look tired and discouraged. They pass me again within the mile, but by early afternoon I find them stretched out on the ground, looking beat. This is harder than they anticipated, they admit, and one of the two is hurting pretty bad—back pain, she says. They've talked it over and come to a Santa Cruz–style solution—they're going to take a day off and fast for twenty-four hours. I never see them again.

I plod on, my energy fading. I resort to my generational solution: not fasting but a combination of ibuprofen and peanut M&Ms. Part of yesterday's success, I admit to myself, came from being focused on a clear goal—getting up the big hill. Nonetheless, by early afternoon I've made my way to Marie Lake, a large body of water at the northern foot of Selden Pass. I could camp at this handsome place, but now that I can see the pass I muster the energy to make the final short climb up a sequence of switchbacks. From a distance, Selden Pass seems to occupy a broad gap between the twelve-thousand-foot-high summits of Mount Hooper and Mount Senger. Up close I find that the trail squeezes through a narrow, rock-lined notch clothed with low thickets of wind-pruned whitebark pine.

Half an hour later I have found a campsite within the low, wind-twisted krummholz forest at Heart Lake. The whitebark pines here, although they cover much of the terrain, are so short that I can see over their crowns when I stand among them. My camp has a great southerly view, and as the light fades I study the revealed landscape. Tomorrow I will make my next big descent, this time into the broad canyon of the South Fork of the San Joaquin River. There I will meet a companion who will join me for the next leg of this journey.

For through-hikers on the Muir Trail, the canyon of the South Fork of the San Joaquin River is a major landmark. For southbound hikers, it holds the last resupply station on or near the trail. The station is accessed via the Florence Lake Ferry, a water taxi similar to the one at Lake Edison. The John Muir Wilderness boundary rests just above the ferry's up-lake terminus. Five miles farther up the canyon, however, several tracts of private land adjacent to the Muir Trail provide an enclave in the wilderness, with services for hikers and stock parties. These tracts, sold by the government in the nineteenth century before the creation of national forests or wilderness, remain wilderness ranches. Here, I will rendezvous with my friend Armando Quintero.

I arrive first at the best known of these facilities—the Muir Trail Ranch. Located in thick forest near Blaney Hot Springs, the ranch serves both as a resupply point for long-distance hikers and as a destination resort. I walk in the gate and enter a busy scene. A number of cabins provide accommodations for guests who ride in from Florence

Lake. A small log cabin serves as a gift shop, selling souvenir shirts and ball caps for guests and items like moleskin and Advil for hikers. Guests back from a day of horseback exploration turn their animals over to wranglers in the corrals. At a table in front of another building, backpackers sort through food caches they have sent here to pick up.

I take off my pack and enjoy the scene. I poke my head inside the gift shop to inspect the merchandise but conclude that I don't need a denim shirt with an embroidered Muir Trail Ranch logo. Coming back out into the bright sunshine, I run into the establishment's proprietress, a woman of perhaps seventy years with a no-nonsense attitude. She asks what I'm looking for, and I tell her that I'm just taking a curious look at the ranch because it's been a decade since I last walked by. This must not be the right answer, because she now launches into a litany of rules and cautions. I am to stay outside a fenced area within the ranch, she tells me, and avoid going near guest cabins.

It surprises me to be perceived as a threat to law and order. I've reached the age where such moments form mostly distant memories. Indeed, I've noticed in recent years that neither cops nor younger women take notice of me at all. At Muir Trail Ranch, however, I am somehow dangerous in at least a minor way. Trying to resolve this surprisingly contentious situation, I tell my stern friend that I'll be on my way. In fact, I'm headed to a neighboring ranch, and since I can see the gate a hundred yards away that leads in that direction, I'll happily pass through it and leave her domain.

"Not so fast," she announces, "you can't go that way." I explain, to no avail, that I know where I'm going and it's just down the trail past that gate. Her response (What did I do to this woman?) is that I will have to go out the way I came in and walk around the perimeter of Muir Trail Ranch. Twenty minutes later, having climbed over a hill and come down again, I am outside the forbidden gate and on my way.

I approach Lost Valley Ranch with curiosity. Gene Rose, an old friend and Sierra Nevada historian, has arranged hospitality for me at this property that is closed to the public all but two weeks each year. During those two July weeks, the Ross family operates Lost Valley as an Elderhostel camp in a truly exquisite wilderness setting, offering two weeklong sessions of camping and educational activities for twenty-five lucky Elderhostel participants. The rest of the summer, Lost Valley is the Ross family retreat. This summer's Elderhostel sessions ended several weeks earlier, but my friend has arranged an invitation for me to visit the property and meet the Ross family. Sometime this afternoon, Armando will meet me here as well.

I pass through an outside gate and follow the trail across a meadow. Soon I spy a two-story house, about the same time that several dogs sense my approach. They raise a noisy ruckus. A lanky figure appears on the second-story porch. "You must be Bill Tweed," he says. "Would you like a beer?"

A few minutes later, Lloyd Holland stands in front of his propane range, grilling a frozen salmon patty. Removing the patty from the grill, he drops it onto a toasted bun, adds mayonnaise and avocado, and serves it up on a dinner plate. While I attack this unexpected culinary windfall, Lloyd tells me the story of Lost Valley. Fred Ross, his father-in-law, purchased the property in about 1940. In the years that followed, the Ross family operated a pack station at the upper end of Florence Lake and used the ranch as a destination camp for clients. Over time, operation of the pack station business shifted from Fred to his grown children. In recent years that second generation, now aging as well, decided to phase out the packing business and focus on developing Lost Valley as an Elderhostel destination.

Penny, Lloyd's wife, has returned to her winter job as a teacher, but Lloyd has stayed on, watching over the property until the hiking season ends and working on several minor construction projects. He seems happy to have company. He gets more when Armando arrives.

I've known Armando for a quarter century. I first met him when I hired him for a summer ranger job. After two summers at Sequoia he moved on to a twenty-year career with the Park Service in Northern California. More recently, he has spent his time as an artist, musician, photographer, and dedicated dad of two school-age daughters. Armando and I have hiked together repeatedly over the years, exploring the Sierra. During those hikes I've found him to be almost the perfect wilderness companion, even though he's nearly a decade younger than I am and a good deal faster on the trail. I'm looking forward to having him with me for the next ten days. I'm ready for some company and conversation.

We spend a pleasant afternoon within the quiet confines of Lost Valley. Armando fishes while I shower and sort and repack. Lloyd returns to the kitchen, and soon we're all dining on his second-story balcony, trading Sierra stories. Armando spies a guitar and, using the neck of a Pacifico beer bottle, introduces Lloyd to the secrets of slide guitar technique.

Lloyd has provided luxurious quarters for the night. I enjoy a three-sided, wood-floored shelter complete with a double bed and a propane lamp. As the evening winds down, I return to the shelter, light the lamp, slip into my sleeping bag, and listen to the quiet murmurs of the San Joaquin River.

Many of us come into the wilderness in search of solitude, yet our best wilderness memories often revolve around the people we meet. Perhaps we can't fully appreciate humanity until we reduce it to a few individuals in settings that allow us to talk long enough to get to know each other. Our daily urban lives, full as they are of schedules and entertainments, offer few such opportunities, but my evening at Lost Valley reminds me yet again that wilderness teaches us as much about humanity as it does about nature.

TWO

Kings Canyon National Park

Artwork by Matthew J. Rangel, from *a transect—due east*

Lloyd insists on sending us off with a hot breakfast, so we feast on eggs, sausage, and pancakes in Lloyd's pine-paneled upstairs apartment. After dining, we finish packing. I go through my pack one last time, still searching for more weight to discard. When I'm done, despite second thoughts, I still have several luxuries, including my teapot. I will continue to carry a heavy pack, and I can blame no one but myself.

The morning passes quickly. The trail follows the river up the broad canyon of the San Joaquin, and as we walk Armando and I catch up on events of the past few weeks. After ninety miles of solo hiking I am reminded this morning of how much human company and conversation ease the passage of time on the trail. We talk of my trip to date, families at home, progress at a nonprofit we both support, and plans for the days and miles ahead. Almost before we know it, we arrive at the confluence of Piute Creek with the South Fork of the San Joaquin. A steel-framed trail bridge spans the still-surging creek. At the far end of the bridge, a small metal sign welcomes us to Kings Canyon National Park.

Kings Canyon remains the least known of California's eight national parks. Even fewer of those people who love such places have a complete idea of its glories. Having spent decades exploring this park, I know why so few understand it. To a degree almost unmatched by other national parks in the forty-eight contiguous states, Kings Canyon is a wilderness park. From the time of its creation in 1940, the great majority of its lands have been accessible only by trail. The park consists of two separate tracts. One, the small part most visitors see, features giant sequoia trees. That section, originally set aside in 1890 as General Grant National Park, is accessible by road and seems to most visitors merely an extension of the adjoining Sequoia National Park. The rest of the park—the other 90 percent—preserves the scenic climax of the Sierra Nevada.

Although this section of the park contains almost seven hundred square miles of wonderful scenery, only one tiny portion of this rugged wonderland has ever welcomed a road, and that route penetrates only a few miles up one canyon, to a trailhead. People who know the High Sierra know that it takes a lot of time to see Kings Canyon National Park. Trails lead to nearly every corner of this vast park. Tying them together north to south is the John Muir Trail. From Piute Creek in the north to Forester Pass in the south, it takes the Muir Trail nearly eighty miles to traverse the length of this grand parkland. As Armando and I step off the bridge at Piute Creek and into the park, these miles stretch before us.

From the moment we enter the park, the scenery feels novel, distinctly different from the Forest Service country to the north. A look at the map explains why. Thus far in the San Joaquin River country, the Muir Trail has stayed well away from the Sierra crest. Instead of seeking out the highest peaks and passes, it has followed a route farther west that has allowed it to avoid the most difficult terrain. Now, as Armando and I begin our southerly hike through Kings Canyon Park, the Muir Trail turns up-canyon. For the next two days we will ascend closer and closer to the peaks that form the Sierra's backbone. Once we reach the high peaks, our route will continue south almost always within a few miles of the crest of the range. As we cross Muir, Mather, Pinchot, and Glenn passes, all of them close to twelve

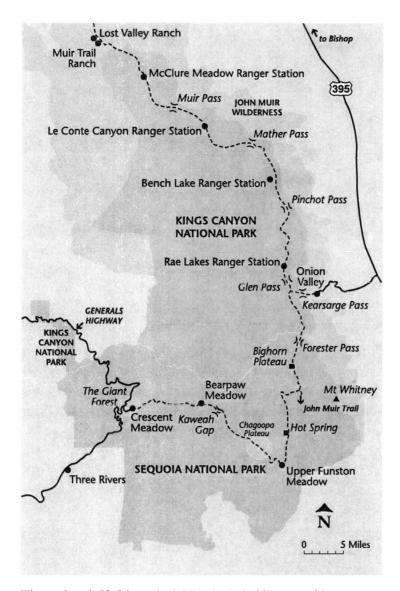

The southern half of the author's hike: the dashed line traces his progress
along the John Muir Trail southward through Kings Canyon National Park
and into northeastern Sequoia National Park, where he turned west on the
High Sierra Trail to complete his trek at Crescent Meadow.

thousand feet above the sea, we will be teased continuously with vistas of yet higher summits, many of them thirteen thousand and even fourteen thousand feet high.

Our gateway to this new world is the canyon of the South Fork of the San Joaquin River. Above its confluence with Piute Creek, the San Joaquin no longer occupies the wide glacial valley that provided space for the Lost Valley and Muir Trail ranches. Just above the park's entrance, the canyon narrows into a rugged V-shaped gorge. The trail hugs the left bank, often cut into hard rock and then supported by masonry held in place with rusty steel pins made from old rock-drill bits. In one place a huge avalanche-generated wedge of snow still buries the shady side of the canyon. When it first plunged into the canyon last winter, the avalanche must have blocked the river to a depth of fifty feet or more.

By midafternoon we've come to a major junction in this scenic gorge. The South Fork of the San Joaquin River, coming now from the south, descends from Mount Goddard, which rises to 13,568 feet. That peak, however, does not grace the Sierra crest. To get closer to the highest peaks, the Muir Trail must ascend Evolution Creek, an easterly tributary of the San Joaquin. This stream drains Evolution Basin, a severe and starkly beautiful alpine bowl dominated by 13,710-foot Mount Mendel and 13,831-foot Mount Darwin. Our route to these heights will take us first through Evolution Valley. Sierra hikers know the "Evolution country" as one of the ultimate wilderness destinations in the range. Not since Thousand Island Lake and Mount Ritter have I approached such storied terrain.

The next morning charms us. Pleistocene glaciers scoured this country and left the mouth of Evolution Valley "hanging" some eight hundred feet above the San Joaquin River. As the first light of a new day spills into the San Joaquin's canyon, we climb granite switchbacks up steep, juniper-graced bluffs to the mouth of this side canyon. Within the hour, we enter Evolution Valley, the first upward step in the giant mountain staircase that will lead us to Muir Pass. We take off our boots and wade thirty-foot-wide Evolution Creek. Then Evolution Meadow comes into view. These biology-based appellations date back to 1895, when Theodore Solomons, a young mountaineer from San Francisco, named the six dominant peaks in the region after the famous evolutionary biologists of the nineteenth century: Darwin, Fiske, Haeckel, Huxley, Spencer, and Wallace. Solomons found his way here pursing his personal dream of defining a trail route that would allow recreationists, including members of the newly founded Sierra Club, to travel through the high country from Yosemite Valley to Kings Canyon, a concept that eventually became the John Muir Trail.[1] In naming the "Evolution Group" of peaks, Solomons set a theme for the entire watershed. In the years that followed, his theme inspired additional names, such as Evolution Meadow, Evolution Valley, Evolution Creek, and Evolution Basin. Appropriately, Mount Darwin, with its distinctive summit plateau, rises a bit taller than the others.

Evolution Meadow is the first of several grand meadows that punctuate the forested floor of Evolution Valley. As we wander through the lodgepole pine forest that leads to the next of these meadows, we encounter three Asian American men in their midtwenties. The three appear well equipped but seem confused. Where, they ask, is the McClure Meadow Ranger Station? The lead hiker explains that they came in via a cross-country route, and that one of their party is having trouble with his boot. Armando and I have no trouble seeing what's wrong: the sole of the unfortunate hiker's boot flaps loosely with each step he takes. We tell them that the ranger station is up-canyon a mile or so in the very direction they are coming from. They've been up that way, they explain, but found a fence and a locked gate blocking their way.

Straightening all this out takes a few minutes. These young men, obviously well-educated and capable (they have successfully navigated a difficult cross-country crossing of the Sierra crest), nonetheless have little understanding of what goes on in the Sierra's recreational wilderness. We explain to them the concept of a "drift fence," yet another of the many compromises made to facilitate enjoyment of these busy recreational wilderness lands. Erected at geographical pinch points along the trails, drift fences retard the nocturnal wanderings of free-grazing horses and mules, making them easier to catch in the morning.

When we arrive at the closed gate, we look at it through the eyes of our newly met companions. The wire fence and gate, obviously human-made intrusions in a land managed so that, as prescribed by the Wilderness Act, "the imprint of man's work is substantially unnoticeable," offer no explanation to those who might not understand them. A sign reading "Please Close the Gate" leaves its purpose undefined. I can come up with no reason why our new friends should have understood this mysterious gate and the fact that it was never intended to prevent their passage.

Future support for the Sierra's wilderness lands will depend on young persons like these three. So much about them encourages me, including their generational identity, their being representatives of a demographic group that seldom uses wilderness, and their obvious willingness to undertake a challenging adventure. With only a map for a guide, these three found their way over some of the highest peaks in the United States. But what have we done on the ground to teach them about wilderness and how it works? Not much, apparently. Old Sierra hands have spent lifetimes opening and shutting drift fence gates. To these three, however, schooled not in wilderness but in modern American culture, the fence delivers a clear message of exclusion. Like so many recreational pursuits, wilderness travel can turn into an insiders' club, an activity comfortable only for those in the know.

Armando and I explain the purpose of the gate and show the young backpackers that it is not actually locked. A few minutes later the five of us arrive at McClure Meadow, and there, sitting on the bedrock ledge in front of his ranger station, drinking tea with his wife, is wilderness ranger George Durkee. I can't call George and Paige close friends, but we've crossed paths and shared pleasant conversations numerous times in three decades of working together in Sequoia and Kings Canyon National Parks. During those years, I started as a seasonal ranger and worked my way into permanent employment and eventually park management. George, truer to his calling, stuck to what he loves best: spending his summers protecting the wilderness of the southern Sierra. As he sees us approach, he rises to his full height of well over six feet and greets us. I say hello, and he recognizes me despite my hat and dark glasses. "I heard you were headed our way," he announces in his unrushed manner. "And who do you have here with you?"

I introduce Armando, then turn George's attention to our companions and the problem of the failing boot. George has obviously seen this minor crisis many times and shifts easily into ranger-cobbler mode. Using duct tape, George reattaches the errant sole and explains what it will take to keep it connected long enough to get its owner back to civilization. He issues the hiker a remnant roll of government-issue tape. All the while he unobtrusively converses, filling in some of the gaps in what these three know about wilderness.

By the time the boot is stabilized and the three are ready to leave, they understand a good deal more about backcountry stock-users, drift fences, and national park wilderness. The three backpackers look like they've made a new friend, and George has once again worked his subtle educational magic. The three resume their trek, heading north.

His duties complete for the moment, George sprawls again on the granite outcrop in front of his tiny log cabin station. Paige serves lemonade, and we chat. The conversation wanders from mosquitoes (fading, at last), to parties of stock users (few so far this year, since Muir Pass is still blocked by snow), to the recovery of the body of an unfortunate hiker who was swept away while bathing in the San Joaquin River earlier in the summer. I catch up on backcountry gossip. Park crews have made some improvements this summer on the McClure station, and George shows off his new storage cabinets and proudly points out new sill logs replacing several that had rotted out in the cabin's log walls. Despite the recent work, George's combination office, headquarters, and residence still contains barely two hundred square feet of interior space, with much of that occupied by cabinets and emergency equipment for search-and-rescue and medical activities. In reality, George and Paige live mostly outdoors and use the cabin primarily for storage.

Over the next few weeks I will visit five more of these remote stations. The men and women who work in them have some of the most sought-after summer jobs in the national park system. Seasonal wilderness rangers at Sequoia and Kings Canyon work for no more than four or five months each year; live in remote locations in primitive shelters, including tents; supply all their own food, and earn a salary less than a beginning schoolteacher's. They receive no health insurance. Despite these limitations, idealistic applicants line up and wait their turn for these jobs. Once obtained, such positions are often jealously protected for years. George, now recognized as the "dean" of the wilderness ranger corps in the two parks, has been at this for more than thirty summers.

Finishing our conversation, Armando and I say good-bye to George and Paige and make our way down to the wet edge of McClure Meadow. The ranger station occupies a forested bench perhaps seventy-five yards from the open edge of the meadow. Below the cabin, a rib of granite forms a small dry peninsula in a sea of flooded marsh. In years past, hikers camped here among the small cluster of trees, but the site could not sustain such intensive use, and the Park Service eventually closed the campsite. The view remains unblemished. In the foreground, Evolution Creek scribes a graceful arc through the wet meadow. Looking to the southeast, we see the polished granite walls of Evolution Valley, the rim of Evolution Basin a thousand feet higher, and then, perfectly framed, the majestic mass of Mount Darwin, rising to 13,831 feet above the sea.

· · ·

The trail leads us several easy miles through the uppermost part of Evolution Valley and then reaches the foot of next big step in this huge scenic staircase. For the next hour we grind up steep switchbacks as we ascend toward Evolution Basin. This "Evolution country"—valley, basin, creek, meadow, lake, and peaks—cannot help but prompt once again the question of change in the natural world and its relationship to national parks and wilderness. Irony abounds here. We humans have taken this spectacular watershed, christened it with names that celebrate the inescapable process that endlessly changes life on our planet, and then placed it under management that seeks to prevent change to the greatest degree possible. Friends in the Park Service have pointed out that, by managing this land as we do, with a strong emphasis on preservation, we restrain humankind's often deleterious effects on the biological world, and that this allows natural processes like evolution to continue. I grant the truth in this assertion, but the relationship between change and the national park system is neither so simple nor so completely positive as this answer suggests.

Like all good ideas, the national park concept itself has evolved. The idea of setting aside large tracts of wildlands with the goal of preserving them in a natural state for public enjoyment dates back to the middle years of the nineteenth century. The concept can be found in its nascent form in the Yosemite Grant of 1864 and comes into better focus in the legislation creating Yellowstone National Park in 1872 and Sequoia, Yosemite, and General Grant National Parks in 1890. The core idea embedded in that pioneer legislation has proven intellectually powerful, leading not only to the still-continuing enlargement of America's national park system but also to the creation of similar reservations in many of the world's nations.

Like all ideas, the national park concept reflects the intellectual perspectives of its time, and this brings us to the idea's relationship to science and to concepts of biological change. The mission of the early national parks, Sequoia and Yosemite among them, rested firmly on a nineteenth-century view of the biological world. As seen through the eyes of taxonomists, then the dominant force in the biological sciences, the natural world consisted of independent species and distinct landscapes. The concept of ecology, the idea that organisms and landscapes often depend on each other for survival, did not appear until the early years of the twentieth century and was not widely appreciated until after 1950. Further contributing to this late-nineteenth-century mind-set is the fact that biological scientists played no significant role in either defining the National Park Service's mission as codified in 1916 or managing the agency in the formative decades after it was created. Instead, the early NPS absorbed without question the cultural assumptions that had driven early park legislation, including the Virgin Continent view of North America and its wildlands.

Out of this mind-set blossomed an idea so simple and powerful that it lives on today: that we can take a piece of land, set it aside within a "fence of laws," and expect it to remain intact and unchanged forever. In this view, the primary threats come from the direct actions of human beings on the land itself. In the Sierra Nevada, for example, if park managers control destructive land uses such as hunting, logging, and grazing, and if they insist that visitors behave respectfully, then the landscape and its special features will endure "unimpaired for the enjoyment of future generations." Nearly a century after its formulation, and despite much scientific evidence to the contrary, this idea continues to widely hold sway with the public and many NPS employees.

Initially, the Park Service pursued this vision by implementing a strategy of preserving visual integrity. The early national park movement may have been deficient in scientists, but it contained a significant number of landscape architects. These practitioners of the art of landscape design played important roles in everything from early management of the Yosemite Grant during the 1860s to the campaign to create the Park Service that succeeded in 1916. Once the agency came to life after the First World War and began to hire professional staff, the service created it own internal corps of landscape architects. A clear assumption dominated their work: that parklands could be trusted to remain healthy and natural if they *appeared* healthy and natural.[2]

This visual paradigm permeated the management of the national parks from the founding of the agency in 1916 to the early 1960s. During this era, the service's landscape architects, a committed band of visionaries, created some of the nation's best-loved built environments. They even invented a distinctive national park architecture based on the exaggerated use of natural materials like stone and rough timber and regional historical tradition. It is not too much to assert that this cadre of professionals, schooled in a nature-based discipline that emphasized visual quality, played a central role in the public success of the national park system in the early twentieth century. Much of the political support for national parks that blossomed during the Mather-Albright era resulted from public appreciation of the managed environments designed by the agency's landscape architects.³ What the landscape architects could not ensure, of course, was the actual biological health of park ecosystems.

One of these landscape architects, Conrad Wirth, rose to become director of the agency and remained in that position from 1951 until 1964. Ironically, it was during Wirth's long term that circumstances conspired to provide the Park Service with a radically updated interpretation of its land management mission. By the early 1960s, with a major reconstruction of the park system's physical facilities well under way, the question of modernizing the service's resource management policies became inescapable. The gap between the service's nineteenth-century mission and the burgeoning world of ecological science demanded a reassessment.

In response, Secretary of the Interior Stewart Udall, himself a breath of fresh air in the traditionally stolid halls of the Interior Department, commissioned two outside studies of the service's resources management policies and program. Both the Leopold Report, formally titled "Wildlife Management in the National Parks," and the report on Park Service research activities that was produced by the National Academy of Sciences appeared in 1963. Both challenged the service to make significant changes in its worldview.[4]

The Leopold Report, the result of an effort chaired and guided by A. Starker Leopold of the University of California, proposed that the NPS shift its decision-making process for resolving resource questions from visual management to a scientific approach that incorporated an ecological view. Significantly, Leopold did not challenge the Virgin Continent concept. Indeed, he specifically endorsed it when he defined the mission of the parks as preserving landscapes as they were when first encountered by Euro-American pioneers. The National Academy effort, chaired by William Robbins, led to similar conclusions but focused more specifically on the role of scientific research in achieving these goals. Out of these reports, after much internal debate, came the concept of utilizing "natural processes" as a management strategy. This approach proposed that the key to preserving national park landscapes and ecosystems would be found in natural agents like fire, flood, and critical biological cycles. If the processes that determined the character of the landscape were protected and perpetuated, then the integrity of the landscape could be expected to endure.[5]

Now, half a century later, the Park Service again faces the necessity of paradigm change. Anthropological and historical research have demonstrated the bankruptcy of the Virgin Continent worldview, and numerous ecological studies suggest that humanity has modified the planet so profoundly that *natural results* (an increasingly uncertain concept) can no longer be expected to result inevitably from attempts to perpetuate or mimic natural processes. Yet, even today both the Virgin Continent and natural processes/natural results doctrines remain deeply embedded within the service's collective psyche. The 2006 revision of the agency's *Management Policies*, completed after considerable public dispute, still specifically calls for the agency to protect not only *all* aspects of a park's natural biodiversity but also "the processes that sustain them."[6] The same policy document reminds all park managers that significant impairment or derogation of park resources can be allowed only if specifically authorized by Congress, and that visitor use must always remain subordinate to resource preservation.

These idealistic policies form the bedrock upon which the National Park Service erects the remainder of its natural resources management structure. The policies have strong historical roots and broad public and agency support. They also appear, increasingly, to be unsustainable. Preserving everything no longer seems possible. Even more worrisome is what will happen to national parks as it becomes apparent even to those who love them that the park managers cannot achieve the goals that all have endorsed and defended for decades.

Armando and I reach the uppermost switchbacks and gain our first view of the stark timberline splendor of Evolution Basin. Before us, at an elevation of more than 10,800 feet, shimmers Evolution Lake, a narrow body of water almost a mile long and surrounded by polished rock and small tundra meadows of sedge and wildflowers. To the east tower the crags of the two grand peaks named after Darwin and Mendel, both nearly 14,000 feet high. Despite their size, the big mountains are intimately close. The summits of Darwin and Mendel rise so precipitously that boulders loosened by winter frost from their upper slopes tumble downward across the trail to the very shore of the lake.

Everything in this landscape screams change. Less than fifteen thousand years ago—a microsecond on the geological time scale—glacial ice thousands of feet deep covered everything here but the summits of the highest peaks. In quick succession, over succeeding recent millennia, the ice melted, plants and animals colonized the landscape, and human beings arrived seeking sustenance. The climate warmed and cooled; human cultures ebbed, flowed, and changed. New people arrived, first to map the landscape and seek wealth but soon purely for the pleasure that the country offered. Along the way the region came to carry the name of the most elegant and far-reaching form of biological change yet discovered.

We camp two miles farther into the basin at Sapphire Lake, a rock-rimmed, icy body of water nearly eleven thousand feet high. We may be in California, but we have climbed so high that the landscape could easily be part of Greenland. No trees grow here, and repeated glaciations have left this landscape almost devoid of soil. The calendar tells us that we have arrived in late summer, yet last winter's snowbanks still cling to the ridges that surround us. When the sun disappears behind the ridge to the west, we put on additional layers of clothing. Tonight will be cold.

As the light fades, the granite bedrock that surrounds Sapphire Lake dims to a uniform gunmetal gray. The lake reflects the pale blue of the fading sky. Cool colors accentuate this cold land's essence. But then, just as we assume that the evening's character has resolved itself, everything changes. The sun, making its final approach to the hidden western horizon, drops into the particulate smog of California's lowlands and floods our alpine world with rich, fulvous luminescence. This light illuminates the summits of Mounts Spencer, Haeckel, Wallace, Fiske, and Huxley, and in reflected response the surface of Sapphire Lake catches fire. The lake, cold blue only a moment before, shifts from its namesake gemstone tint to rose-colored diamond. Still locked in a somber setting of shaded granite, this newly warmed gemstone of a lake glows with unanticipated warmth. Cold winds and shivering forgotten, we pull out cameras and attempt to capture the magic of the moment. Ten minutes later, the first bright planets appear in the darkening, high-altitude sky.

. . .

Sierra passes come in many flavors. Some occupy narrow ridges, others occupy broad expanses of barren alpine terrain. Muir Pass falls into this second category. The Muir Trail stays above tree line here for seven or eight miles, one of the longest such stretches on the entire route. This barren upland both exhilarates and daunts us.

Lakes named after John Muir's two daughters, Wanda and Helen, flank the northern and southern approaches to 11,955-foot Muir Pass. As we parallel the eastern shore of Wanda Lake, Muir Pass itself becomes visible. Tucked in a huge U-shaped wind gap between Mount Warlow and the Black Giant, the pass staggers us with its grandeur. Judging the scale of the scene proves impossible until we pick out a beehive-shaped pile of stones crowning the ridge. From a distance it looks like a small cairn, but I know it's a building, a dome of native stone that stands more than twenty feet tall. The Muir Hut rests in lonely splendor among the barren mountains. Its odd design mimics a vernacular architecture developed centuries ago by Italian shepherds who, when faced with the challenge of building without access to timber, roofed their circular shelters with such domes. Using this same design, the Sierra Club erected the Muir Hut in 1930 to provide shelter for travelers caught by weather or bad timing in this barren and often inhospitable upland.

On the John Muir Trail, at Muir Pass, while sitting on the stone steps of the Muir Hut, I find it obligatory to ponder the contributions of the ubiquitous Scotsman to the world of national parks and wilderness. No other historical figure is so closely associated with the Sierra Nevada.

A native of Scotland who spent much of his youth on frontier homesteads in Wisconsin, Muir first arrived in these mountains in 1868. He never really left. As late as 1913, the year before his death, he was deeply immersed in an unsuccessful campaign to block the damming and flooding of Hetch Hetchy Valley in Yosemite National Park. A century later, Muir's name graces more California features and facilities than that of any other person. California contains not only fourteen-thousand-foot Mount Muir, adjacent to Mount Whitney, but also Muir Grove, Muir Gorge, and a national monument named Muir Woods. His name identifies schools, city parks, and hospitals. Muir was even given the ultimate California accolade, a freeway named after him. The man seems to be everywhere, but why?

In his nearly fifty years as a Californian, Muir accomplished two things of enduring value for all who love wildness and the national parks. First, better than any other public figure of his time, he anticipated the significance of wildlands to an urbanizing nation. While most nineteenth-century Californians saw the Sierra as a land waiting to be "developed" by loggers, ranchers, and miners, Muir saw instead a romantic world of beauty and escape for a quickly urbanizing population. It could be said that he anticipated modern tourism, although much about the way we pursue it today would not enthuse him.

The other reason we remember Muir is that he wrote. During the last twenty years of his nearly eight-decade-long life, he laboriously drafted a series of popular and enduring books that still capture the essence of the Sierra's wild beauty. *My First Summer in the Sierra, The Mountains of California,* and *Our National Parks* all describe the Sierra at length, as do many of his other books and magazine articles.

Trained in his Scottish youth to appreciate literary sources as varied as Milton, the King James Bible, and the songs and poems of Robert Burns, Muir wrote in a flowery nineteenth-century style that differs significantly from modern prose. But his strong images and telling detail make his writing readable, and it is still commonly read today. All who care about nature and the Sierra Nevada eventually read major portions of Muir's works, and most come away inspired by both the depth of his passion for nature and the beauty of what he termed his "scribblings." For many, he has become the secular patron saint of the Sierra, a semimythical figure with a reputation that approaches that of Saint Francis.

But unlike most saints, Muir, especially in his last years, immersed himself deeply in politics and controversy. Seeking to protect the natural beauty he thought so important, he lobbied presidents, organized campaigns for legislation, and led the effort to create the Sierra Club, initially to encourage wildland recreation. These efforts made him enemies. During the fight over Hetch Hetchy, a San Francisco newspaper published an editorial cartoon depicting Muir as a cranky old man holding a broom and trying to sweep back the inevitable tide of progress.

Muir saw science through distinctly nineteenth-century lenses, yet his natural curiosity and penchant for careful observation brought him up against the interconnected nature of what we now call ecology. This did not persuade him, however, to question the assumptions of his time about how wildlands might best be preserved. Muir's concerns about land management centered on the consumption and destruction of forests, meadows, and wildlife. He railed against logging and the wildland grazing of cattle and sheep and saw the creation of federal reserves as the best deterrent to destruction.

Many have interpreted Muir's idealization of nature in pantheistic terms, as almost a form of worship. There is logic to this. Muir spent his youth among stern Calvinists, whose outlook conflicted sharply with his sense that the world was full of beauty and joy. He rebelled and found his own religion, although he did not call it that. In his belief that nature deserved to be preserved for its beauty, and that such beauty could provide important escape for urban people, Muir helped lay down key principles that still inspire us in our approach to national parks and wilderness today.[7]

Sitting in the sun at Muir Pass, Armando and I discuss all this with some curious hikers who have joined us. Two German brothers, in particular, know relatively little about the Sierra's secular Scottish saint. They ask the inevitable question: Did Muir come here? Ironically, there is no evidence that Muir ever visited the pass that now bears his name. Although he wandered widely over the Sierra, especially during the 1870s, he never explored the remote country that separates the San Joaquin and Kings Rivers. That task fell instead to Theodore Solomons and a young University of California professor named J. N. Le Conte.

Leaving the Muir Hut, we enter the world that bears Le Conte's name. In the next half dozen miles we will descend more than three thousand feet as we drop into Le Conte Canyon. Gravel switchbacks lead down the south side of the pass. We drop a few hundred vertical feet into a stark basin closely confined by glacier-sculpted thirteen-thousand-foot peaks. In this place of rock and snow, numerous trickles and rivulets come together to form the source of the Middle Fork of the Kings River, one of the Sierra's grandest and wildest seasonal torrents.

Helen Lake, named for Muir's younger daughter, occupies the lowest end of the basin but is still 11,617 feet above the sea. We're in the last week of August, but huge snowbanks still block the trail. In rocky draws (Muir would have called them "glens"), fresh sprouts of green poke upward from soil just exposed to the warmth of the sun by the continuing snowmelt. With September only a few days off, and the days shortening quickly as the equinox approaches, the basin's plant life enjoys only the shortest of summers.

Our goal tonight lies deep in the heart of Le Conte Canyon. The uppermost portion of the canyon consists of a series of giant downward steps, each defined by small basins and meadows and punctuated by rocky drops of several hundred feet. In one of these basins not far below tree line, I spy a cluster of tents surrounded by more containers and equipment than backpackers usually carry. I know what this camp is about. We've arrived at the Le Conte frog camp. Here, a NPS research crew works to understand why mountain yellow-legged frogs have almost disappeared from the High Sierra.

As late as the 1970s, huge numbers of mountain yellow-legged frogs occupied the high country of the Sierra Nevada. Small ponds and streams often teemed with them. The three-inch-long amphibians were so common that few of us paid much attention to them. I remember the year they began to disappear. In the summer of 1983, after a particularly heavy winter, frog populations crashed in several popular alpine areas in the western part of Sequoia National Park. We had no idea what had happened to them.

In the 1990s, as frogs disappeared from site after site, the NPS set out to discover the reason. Scientists developed several theories. One proposed that introduced trout were preying on frog eggs and tadpoles so effectively that frogs had been extirpated from nearly all lakes and streams with fish. To test this hypothesis, the NPS set out to remove trout from an area—the upper reaches of Le Conte Canyon—that still had remnant frog populations and study the results. This experiment continues today. Using gill nets, the NPS spent several summers removing all trout from the highest head-waters of the South Fork of the Kings River. As the fish disappeared, frog numbers increased. Hundreds could be seen where only a few had hung on a few years earlier.

Removing trout, it turns out, did allow frog populations to rebound. But soon a new problem developed, and frog mortality increased again. Further research disclosed that a fungal disease spread by humans was killing frogs in many areas, including the High Sierra. To make matters worse, high levels of agricultural pesticides have been measured in these high country lakes, and these chemicals also apparently have contributed to the collapse of frog populations. For the moment, Le Conte's frogs are surviving, but their future is far from certain. The High Sierra, with its multiple national parks and wilderness areas, still may not be big enough to protect these fragile amphibians from the effects of human activity.[8]

Like most of the other wilderness stations in Kings Canyon National Park, the Le Conte Canyon Ranger Station has nothing pretentious about it. Tucked among lodgepole pines at an altitude of about nine thousand feet, the one-room wooden frame structure encloses a bit more space than George Durkee's tiny station at McClure Meadow, but even so it offers its occupant only minimal shelter.

Ranger Dave Gordon greets us by name with a confidence that

tells us that George passed news over the park's backcountry radio system of our intended route. I don't know Dave as well as I know George. Although Dave is yet another baby-boomer ranger, he has come to this work only in recent years after a career as a civil engineer. He brings to the wilderness the passion of a man who has found the joy and excitement in his second career that had faded from his earlier endeavors. Gordon welcomes us to the small dirt plaza in front of his humble office-home, brings several folding chairs out of the cabin, and hands us each a can of beer.

We begin with the usual trail talk. Armando and I report on the condition of the remaining snowbanks on Muir Pass. Dave tells us about the summer's events in nearby Dusy Basin and Le Conte Canyon. Taking in our weary and battered condition, he invites us to set up our tents near the station and shares the welcome news that his solar shower is full of hot water. I grab my skimpy synthetic-fiber towel and head into the woods in search of the shower. I find the black plastic bladder resting on a sunny, south-facing rock. Dave must have put it out several hours ago, because it now contains several gallons of sun-heated water. I hang the bladder on a carabiner attached to a pine branch, strip down, and step onto a small plywood platform at the foot of the tree. I twist the small plastic valve open, and a gentle, luxurious shower of hot water emerges.

Feeling much better, I return to the station and extract my food cache from the small storage room tacked on the back of Dave's cabin. I sent these supplies in two months ago, and they've been waiting for me. While Armando goes in search of fish for dinner, I open and sort the contents of my stash. Armando returns in a few minutes with half a dozen eight-inch-long golden trout, a gift from the cold cascades of the Kings River. After cleaning the fish, my fisherman friend concocts a fresh trout curry while Dave mixes up rice and vegetables.

We dine in the cabin sitting in actual chairs around a genuine table while a lantern lights our simple feast.

I move out early the next morning while Armando tarries at the ranger station talking to Dave. Precipitous granite bluffs and receding amphitheaters flank the forested floor of this U-shaped gorge. For the first hour, sun and shadow alternate as I pass below the towering promontories and shadowy recesses that form the canyon's walls. There is a formality and symmetry to this place that feels almost human-made. Several miles pass easily. The trail drifts gently down along the southward-flowing river. I know challenge lies ahead, but for the moment I enjoy Le Conte Canyon.

This place takes its name from Joseph N. ("Little Joe") Le Conte. Like his father before him, Le Conte taught at the University of California. Between the two of them, a Le Conte taught at Cal from 1869 to 1937. The father was a professor of geology and natural history, while the son established himself in the field of engineering mechanics. Both had a special relationship to the Sierra Nevada. Along with Theodore Solomons and the Stanford University art professor Bolton Coit Brown, the younger Le Conte emerged in the 1890s as a key pioneer in the opening of the High Sierra to recreational use. Le Conte explored and mapped much of the Kings River headwaters in those years, laying the foundation for Sierra Club outings in the region after the turn of the century. When Robert Marshall of the United States Geological Survey completed the first topographic map of the Kings River headwaters in 1912, he had labeled it with not only the pass that Marshall named after John Muir but also a canyon memorializing Joseph N. Le Conte's role in opening the country to camping parties.

Few who are familiar with the modern Sierra Club, recognized worldwide for its environmental advocacy, know much of its early history as a California mountaineering club. The contemporary Sierra Club has outgrown its name in many ways, but in its early decades the club did focus closely on the Sierra Nevada. At the time of its founding by John Muir and a number of other like-minded residents of the Bay Area in 1892, the club envisioned its mission as the preservation of the forests and other features of the Sierra Nevada through a program of information, use, and personal enjoyment—a mix that would later be taken up whole by Stephen Mather in his campaign to create the National Park Service.

Pursuing its incorporated purposes "to explore, enjoy, and render accessible the mountain region of the Pacific Coast," the club began in 1901 to organize annual outings that took hundreds of club members into the High Sierra for wilderness camping trips of several weeks' duration. The first of these trips established the campers' base at Tuolumne Meadows in the high country of Yosemite. The following summer, the club set up camp at Copper Creek on the floor of the Kings Canyon. The *Sierra Club Bulletin* annuals for 1902 and 1903 not only documented the adventures of the 1902 outing participants in the high country around Kings Canyon but also contained two long articles by Le Conte summarizing his exploration of the Kings River headwaters.[9]

In 1903, Le Conte pulled together all that was then known about the region and produced a recreational map that covered the high-country basins of the Kings, Kern, and Kaweah rivers. Other maps reflected his explorations in the San Joaquin River headwaters and Yosemite National Park regions. Each map could be obtained from him at the university for $1.50. These maps did more than any other contemporary action to bring to life the Sierra Club's "render accessible" goal. By 1915, when the California Legislature passed the bill that created the John Muir Trail, knowledge of the mountains had advanced to the point that the bill could specify the trail's intended route with useful accuracy. The High Sierra had ceased to be an unknown wilderness.

Following that 1915 route, I arrive at Grouse Meadow, a wet sedge marsh that offers stupendous views of the granite walls that confine the lower reaches of Le Conte Canyon. Looking back up-canyon, I note that the morning sun now fills this grand defile with bright light. Since leaving Muir Pass, I've dropped almost four thousand feet in less than twenty-four hours. Now, in the next twenty-four, I will regain all that altitude as I climb to Mather Pass. It's time to resume the work of climbing big hills.

For the next few miles, the trail ascends the left bank of Palisade Creek, passing through a canyon-bottom landscape with mixed stands of Jeffrey pine, fir, aspen, and sagebrush. Lightning sparked a fire here in the summer of 2002, and the Park Service allowed it to burn. Over a period of more than a month, the fire worked its way through much of the timbered country along the floor of Palisade Creek Canyon, killing a substantial percentage of the canyon's pines and firs. Now the resulting dead snags are collapsing, providing a lot of work for a trail crew. I pass freshly sawn logs, each neatly rolled off the trail. Eventually I catch up with the crew. They're taking a break in the shade of a surviving pine with their chain saws cooling beside them. They look young, dirty, and buff. A summer of this work tunes young bodies to a formidable degree, and these young men and women look as if they could toss rocks and logs off the trail without raising a sweat. I want to tell them to treasure this youthful moment of perfect strength and health, but think better of it and pass them by with only a friendly wave.

The sun is at its zenith when I reach the base of the Golden

Staircase. Unlike many of the other canyons in this rugged country, the gorge of Palisade Creek does not traverse a prolonged series of glacial steps. Instead, this major tributary of the Middle Fork drops abruptly from an upper basin into a lower canyon. A steep thousand-foot climb separates these two worlds: the Golden Staircase. Arriving at the base of this obstacle, I've already climbed more than a thousand feet since leaving the Kings River, but now the canyon narrows and a wall of rock rises before me. The trail, anticipating the obstacles ahead, begins by climbing the talus slope on the left. Soon this angle runs into hard rock, and switchbacks begin.

My two hours on the Golden Staircase bring together the best and worst of wilderness trail travel. The route, steep and rocky, climbs mercilessly through imposing scenery. Just finding a way through this mass of bluffs, cliffs, and talus must have challenged the engineers who laid out this trail seventy years ago. Indeed, this difficult section of the Muir Trail was the last piece of the route to be completed. The trail works its way across the terrain with the grace and assurance of a football quarterback evading tacklers. In rapid succession the granite pathway sprints across a hardrock ledge, dances up a short series of switchbacks, and then cuts back sharply the other direction to move around a steep outcrop. In places, the trail has been carved from hundred-million-year-old granite. Another stretch is nothing more than two parallel rows of boulders defining a route across smooth bedrock. I keep on climbing. To my amazement, I'm still ahead of Armando.

Finally, the terrain begins to change. The route gains the lip of a basin, and the grade eases. I walk out onto a rolling plateau of low sedge and exposed bedrock. Only a handful of stunted timberline trees breaks the openness. Two hundred yards ahead, rock-bound Lower Palisade Lake glistens in the late-afternoon light. To my left, the towering mass of Middle Palisade, 14,012 feet high and barely a mile away, dominates the horizon.

I shed my pack in grateful relief and cast about for a campsite. Several other parties have already staked claims to the better sites, so I settle for a lightly used site in the middle of the open ground, where Armando will soon join me. At least we'll have a view tonight.

. . .

The next morning, we resume our southward march. Today, we must cross 12,100-foot Mather Pass and then spend the afternoon traversing the barren expanse of Upper Basin. We pass by Upper Palisade Lake, well below us, and we enter again the barren, rocky world that defines the true High Sierra. Armando moves ahead, and I turn my thoughts to Stephen Mather, the man whose legacy this pass commemorates.

In the mythology of national parks, Stephen Mather ranks as a protohero. This founding father not only successfully managed the 1915–1916 campaign to create the National Park Service but also served for a dozen years as the agency's first director, overseeing the development of its defining policies and management character. Shortly after his death in 1930, memorial plaques were placed to honor his contributions to the national park system. Nearly eighty years later, both Yosemite and Sequoia still maintain these memorials. They read in part: "There will never come an end to the good he has done." To understand national parks, one must understand Steve Mather.

National-park people are so familiar with Mather as founding father that few take the time to notice the many things he was not. Mather made no pretense to being any sort of scientist or academic like Le Conte, nor was he a writer or philosopher like Muir. In his early years, he worked for a spell as a journalist in the rough-and-tumble world of 1880s New York, but it was in 1893, when he joined the Pacific Coast Borax Company, that he found the niche that would make him rich. Mather's role in the borax world focused not on mining or refining the product but on selling it. He invented one of America's best-known brand-names: Twenty Mule Team Borax. Mather, in short, was a marketing genius, and this is what he brought to the national park world when he was recruited in 1915 by Interior Secretary Franklin Lane to manage the campaign to create a bureau of national parks.

Although the Mather family prized its New England roots, Mather was born in California and thought of himself throughout his life as a representative of the Golden State. He attended and received a degree from the University of California and enjoyed many California connections. Through his California friends, he joined the Sierra Club. He participated in its 1912 outing to the Kern River Canyon and then, while visiting the Giant Forest area of Sequoia National Park a few weeks later, encountered John Muir on what would be the older man's last visit to the southern Sierra Nevada. Through these relationships Mather absorbed the key elements of John Muir's and the Sierra Club's view of national parks. If these places were to be preserved successfully, Muir had preached, they would have to be made accessible and enjoyed by the public. To this premise, Mather the adman appended a corollary: *If parks were to be used, they had to be publicized.*

All this came together when Secretary Lane asked Mather to come to Washington for a few months to manage the national parks bureau campaign. By the time the campaign ended successfully, Mather's plans for who would serve as the agency's founding director had fallen apart after acrimonious debate, and Mather decided to stay on and carry out the role himself, aided by his young assistant, Horace Albright. So it came to be that the National Park Service was founded, and then defined and managed in its early years, by an advertising man.[10]

Three-quarters of a century after Mather's death, his philosophies still inform much that defines our national park system. As befits an organization founded by an adman, the Park Service long prided itself on being, according to annual polling, "the most respected agency in the federal government." Today the agency annually surveys its visitors and reports "visitor satisfaction" rates well above 90 percent. Mather would recognize that such accolades reflect a continuation of the focus he established so long ago.

The Park Service markets the parks and the agency in many ways. During my decades with the bureau, I worked in a series of park ranger jobs that had marketing components. At various times I served both as an "interpreter" (a role known in earlier times as "ranger-naturalist") and as a public affairs officer. In these positions I shared the official vision of national parks with park visitors, community neighbors, and media outlets. Regardless of my functional title, the public perceived me in all these roles as simply a "park ranger." Wearing a uniform that included the famous flat-brimmed Stetson hat made me instantly recognizable in that role. Mather the advertising man not only invented the Twenty Mule Team brand for selling borax but also the park-ranger brand for marketing national parks. Rangers had existed before Mather, of course, but he refined and strengthened their role and marketed them as *the* symbol of the national park system. They remain so today.

Marketing involves both image and message, and the Park Service has always emphasized both in its communication programs. Since

I worked in parks that preserved natural landscapes, my jobs came with clearly defined positions (called "talking points" by the agency) on land management issues. Many of these reflected Mather's vision. The first director saw most park problems in political, not ecological, terms. Throughout his dozen years as director, by focusing his attention on marketing the parks and attracting users, he influenced the legislative system to increase funding for staffing and physical improvements like roads, trails, campgrounds, and buildings. Mather's landscape goals concerned things like removing human-made "blights" from the viewshed (legend recounts that he once blew up a visually offensive sawmill in Glacier National Park) and, critically, gaining control of more land for the park system. Mather drove the managers of the national forest system into bitter opposition by his endless determination to grow the western national parks at the expense of their national forest neighbors.

In the tenth decade of national park management by the National Park Service, these historic roots still influence much that the agency pursues. Marketing of the parks and agency remains a major priority. Indeed, in my last years with the service, the agency implemented a major image-renewal effort using the advice of advertising consultants to update and make more consistent its visual identity. Everything from road signs to publications came under review. The agency even selected its own proprietary typeface that was to be used in all its publications. At the same time, despite growing awareness among some of its more informed employees that an environmental crisis loomed, the agency continued to spend the overwhelming majority of its funding on visitor services and visitor-related issues.

In my decades at Sequoia and Kings Canyon, I attempted several times to calculate the percentage of the park budget that went into visitor services and what might be called "visitor mitigation" (programs like removing hazardous trees that threatened to fall on buildings or handling problem bears around campgrounds). Even my most conservative estimates indicated that funding for managing and delivering visitor services and mitigation consumed at least 90 percent of the parks' fiscal resources. Mather has been gone for more than seventy-five years, but his visitor-focused priorities continue to inform his old agency. Such is the power his legacy.

If he were alive today, Mather would argue that, even if scientific knowledge has advanced, it is useful only in a political setting where the public supports its parks. He would be right in this. It is public support for the protection of national parks that has defeated periodic attempts to open the parks to increased commercial use and development. One of these attempts occurred during my last year with the agency, when the political managers of the George W. Bush Interior Department attempted a major revision of the agency's management policies with the goal of opening the parks to, among other things, greatly increased mechanized recreation. The idea collapsed once it fell under public scrutiny. Too many who cared about the parks objected, and the Interior Department backed away from the proposal and allowed a much more traditional set of revisions to be promulgated. Most national park advocates saw the result as a clear victory.

An assault on the national parks had been repulsed, but at the same time an opportunity had been missed. The opening idea advanced by the Interior Department—that national parks must adjust to the different world of the twenty-first century—was not completely mistaken; it was the intended direction that was in error. The proposed revisions failed because they reflected not the need for the parks to respond to a changing world but the hopes of various commercial interests to make more money from the national park "business."

Unfortunately, the winning side in this debate displayed equally limited vision. The ideas that won out centered on the ancient, Mather-era proposition that, if the parks are properly managed internally, they will prosper and remain intact. The winners, in short, defaulted to Stephen Mather's marketing points, and once again Mather's politically astute vision worked its magic. As revised in the summer of 2006, the agency's *Management Policies* still promises that America can both use its national parks in the traditional way and expect to preserve them intact and unchanging forever. In the "Underlying Principles" section of the *Policies*, the service goes so far as to assert that it aims to pass on the natural resources for which it is responsible in even better condition than they are today.[11]

As political marketing, this promise remains enormously potent, but as an expression of environmental reality it reflects a failure to face how profoundly the planet is changing. This continued denial of environmental reality has become the ticking time bomb of the national park world. Stephen Mather's heritage comes with this deep dichotomy. His vision both created the world's best system of national parks and imbued that system with a public image so powerful and successful that it cannot be revised even when the system is in deep trouble.

. . .

Mather Pass behind us, Armando and I spend the afternoon traversing Upper Basin. To the east, less than two miles away, 14,058-foot Split Mountain crowns this section of the Sierra crest. To the west, equally close, we can see Mount Ruskin and Vennacher Needle, the latter a mere 5 feet shy of 13,000 feet. The basin itself is a surprisingly open place, an ice-scraped, tundra world of sky and rock. The trail descends gently to the south, following the crest of a broad, sandy moraine.

Earlier, near Muir Pass, we had witnessed the birth of the Middle Fork of the Kings River. Here, in Upper Basin, we see the first stirrings of what will become the South Fork of the Kings, the other major fork of this river that defines Kings Canyon National Park. Late afternoon has arrived by the time we come to the south end of Upper Basin. The river turns to the west at this point, and we cross it on boulders. Already the South Fork has grown from an inches-wide brook to an energetic stream fifteen feet across. We consider camping here among the lodgepole pines but decide against it. We've grown accustomed to having good evening views, and this place confines us. We resolve to go a bit farther.

An hour of sweat brings us to our destination, a small, unnamed lake situated on a bench above the rim of the canyon. I know this place and have camped here before. I also know that this gentle place comes with stories. As we set up our camp, I think back to a visit I made here twenty-five years earlier. Hiking alone in early October, I arrived here after a day of snow showers. Several inches of snow had already accumulated. I scraped the ground clear, erected my tent, and crawled in for the night. I awoke in the morning to two feet of cold powder and near-gale-force winds. The trail had disappeared overnight under waist-deep snowdrifts. It took me several difficult days to extract myself from this isolated location. I look back on that trip as a true wilderness adventure, an exercise in challenge and self-reliance.

Others, too, have come to grief here. A few hundred yards from tonight's camp, hidden in the trees, stands a summer ranger station maintained by the National Park Service. Named after Bench Lake, a larger body of water two miles to the west, this station consists of a canvas-walled tent erected on a wooden platform, a picnic table, and some metal storage boxes. On the amenities scale for backcountry ranger stations, the Bench Lake Station falls near the bottom. In comparison, the stations at Le Conte Canyon and McClure Meadow, both fully enclosed wooden cabins, seem almost palatial. No one is home tonight; the ranger apparently is out on patrol. That fact evokes another story that still haunts this place.

In July 1996, backcountry ranger Randy Morgenson tied down the flaps of this tent and walked away on a wilderness patrol from which he never returned. Several days passed before his supervisors began to worry about him. At first they assumed he was having radio trouble, but it eventually became apparent that he was missing. The Park Service organized an intensive search and spent several weeks looking for him. Dozens of park staff, working mostly in pairs, climbed high and low over the surrounding several hundred square miles of wilderness searching for some sign of his passing. They found nothing.

Before he disappeared, Morgenson had survived twenty-eight seasons in the wilderness with hardly a scratch. Now he had vanished. A scaled-down search continued the next year and the next. Despite rumors that Morgenson had disappeared on purpose, his fellow rangers, including experienced wilderness hands like George Durkee, remained convinced that his remains were still out there somewhere. Finally, in 2001, trail workers wandering far from any maintained route discovered his pack and radio and a few bones in a rushing stream. In the stream also was his decay-resistant polyester park ranger shirt, complete with badge.

Morgenson's disappearance prompted changes in wilderness operations. Today, backcountry rangers are required to use their radios to stay in much more frequent contact with park headquarters, and they must record and share their intended hiking routes before they set out. They still work alone, however, and still patrol at times far off the trails. The search for Morgenson eventually inspired a book. Eric Blehm's *The Last Season* reads like a novel, and the story has the power of good fiction. The only catch, of course, is that it's all true.[12]

Back in camp after our visit to the lonely ranger tent, Armando and I start dinner. As the stove roars, something in the sky catches our eye. The last two days have been warm and almost cloudless, but looking at the peaks that tower around us, we see that the weather is changing. Streamlined, art-deco-style clouds have formed over the summits, usually a sign that a Pacific low-pressure area has shifted far enough south for a strong westerly wind to begin to flow over the Sierra Crest. As the sun approaches the western horizon, warm reddish light illuminates the lenticular forms in the sky. At the same time, the wind, blowing at some unimaginable strength far above our still lake, tortures and sculpts the clouds into a slow motion ballet of elegant and twisting waves of light. The motion resembles the northern lights, but there is nothing pale or ephemeral about this sky. As the sun drops below the horizon, the bright light moves higher and higher, rising above the summits of the peaks and finally brightening only the tops of the highest clouds. Then, they too begin to fade from glowing red, to purple, to cold blue.

We awaken to clear skies and frost. It's so cold we take a little extra time to get going, waiting for the sun to reach our camp and warm us. The morning's drill is familiar. We begin the climb to Pinchot Pass, yet another twelve-thousand-foot summit. Pinchot Pass and nearby Pinchot Peak memorialize Gifford Pinchot, founder of the United States Forest Service. Little Joe Le Conte first applied the name to the peak in 1902, well before it became apparent that Pinchot and

Le Conte's friend John Muir would come to represent two opposing views of how America's wild landscape should be managed.

The story of these two men in many ways still defines the history of American conservation. Although Muir was a generation older than Pinchot (Muir was born in 1838 and Pinchot in 1865), they both came to be public figures in the last years of the nineteenth century. They had much in common. Both argued that America needed to rethink its relationship with the natural world; both espoused new philosophies for revising that relationship; both sought public support for their causes; and both developed personal relationships with President Theodore Roosevelt. In the end, however, they founded rival traditions that still provide opposing views about humankind's relationship to nature. We have yet to resolve the argument they initiated.

While Muir looked at America's relationship to the natural world and saw greed and damage to nature's cathedral, Pinchot saw something else entirely. To the younger man, what was wrong with America's land management ethics had to do not with lost beauty but with inefficiency and waste. If Muir was a philosopher at heart and almost a mystic, Pinchot was an efficiency expert, a figure who wanted to teach America how to get the most out of its natural resources. By the beginning of the twentieth century, both had focused their attention on the nation's public lands. Muir saw the federal government as an agent that could set aside and protect lands as national parks. Pinchot had something else in mind.

Pinchot graduated from Yale in 1889, and during the following year, while Muir worked to create Yosemite National Park, Pinchot traveled to Germany to study forestry. He was the first American to do so. The very concept of forestry, the idea that forests had to be managed to ensure their long-term productivity, had not yet established roots in North America, where forestlands seemed so vast as to be inexhaustible. By the end of the nineteenth century, however, that sense had begun to fade. The great white pine forests of the Great Lakes region had been harvested, as had the hardwood forests of New England and much of the Appalachians. A great deal of timber remained, especially in the West, but America was ready to consider that the time had come to manage its forests rather than simply consume them.

Imbued with a European version of what later came to be called "the gospel of efficiency," Pinchot returned to the United States and set out to teach his native land about the potential of forestry as a discipline. He worked for several years on private projects, and then, in 1898, obtained the position of head of the Forestry Division in the Agriculture Department. As the federal government's first trained forester, Pinchot played a role that was strictly advisory: no lands came with his new job. All that would change once Theodore Roosevelt moved into the White House.

Vice President Theodore Roosevelt assumed the presidency unexpectedly in 1901 after the assassination of President McKinley. Chosen to run for vice president to balance the Republican Party ticket, Roosevelt had little in common with the conservative party that had elected him. He thought America ripe for change, and he set out to facilitate that change on a massive scale. In Pinchot, Roosevelt found an ally. The two talked at length about what could be done to rationalize America's wildland management, and Pinchot's clear vision convinced the president that a distinct break had to be made with the past. In 1905, by executive order, Roosevelt transferred the existing Forest Reserve system from the Interior Department to the Agriculture Department, where the reserves fell under the control of Gifford Pinchot, the department's resident forester. Pinchot sud-

denly controlled millions of acres of public land, including most of
the Sierra Nevada. He renamed these lands "national forests."

Pinchot knew exactly what he wanted to do with this huge domain.
Over the next several years, he applied his European forestry training to America's public lands on a scale no European could ever
have imagined. In 1907, he issued a small publication titled *The Use
of the National Forests.*[13] Within the thin red volume's forty-two pages,
Pinchot set out a clear vision for managing public lands, not to preserve nature but instead—and much more importantly in his mind—
to meet the needs of a growing and industrializing nation. The caption for the volume's frontispiece said it all. Under a photograph of a
high-altitude ridge covered with trees, the caption read: "A National
Forest which regulates water flow, holds the soil, and furnishes timber
and wood for mining." Even the title of the book made clear Pinchot's
goal, that America's forests were there to be used. Pinchot, as good a
marketer as Mather would be a decade later, named his new public
philosophy "conservation."

Initially, Muir and his Sierra Club allies like Little Joe Le Conte
assumed that Pinchot's evolving philosophies were compatible with
their own. Certainly, they agreed with him that America's use of forest and mountain lands had been destructive and wasteful. It was
during this time, in 1902, that Le Conte named Pinchot Peak. After
1905 and the creation of the Forest Service, fundamental differences
in Muir's and Pinchot's goals emerged. The divergence became fully
visible when the City of San Francisco initiated a campaign to dam
the spectacular Hetch Hetchy Valley in Yosemite National Park for
use as a municipal reservoir. Muir did everything he could to defeat
the proposal, which had the strong support of Pinchot. Muir lost his
campaign for Hetch Hetchy when Congress passed a bill authorizing
a dam there in 1912. But that defeat, along with the increasing power

of the Forest Service and its conservation-for-use philosophy, played a major role in fueling the campaign that brought Stephen Mather to Washington in 1915 and led to the creation of the National Park Service.

In the decades that followed, Mather and his successors fought a continuing bureaucratic war with Pinchot's successors over the fate of many western landscapes. Nowhere was this truer than in the battle over the headwaters of the Middle and South Forks of the Kings River. As early as 1915, even before the campaign for a national parks bureau succeeded, Mather had set his sights on creating what he called a "Greater Sequoia" national park, a much-enlarged reservation that would add the Kings Canyon and Mount Whitney regions to the relatively small existing park. This campaign led to open warfare between the two agencies in the early 1920s.[14]

Looking at the high country of the Kings River watershed, the Forest Service and the Park Service argued for starkly different futures. The Forest Service, which had managed the region since 1905, sought to initiate productive development, including logging, hydroelectric power generation, and irrigation storage. National Park advocates envisioned the region as a grand wilderness park to be maintained in all its primitive beauty. The two agencies fought over this for nearly twenty years.

The Forest Service argued that the two most significant utilitarian resources to be found in the Kings River headwaters country were its water and its potential for hydroelectric power generation. As early as 1920, the City of Los Angeles, having just completed its Owens Valley Aqueduct along the Sierra's east side, began reservoir site surveys in the Kings Canyon high country. Over the next decade, engineers worked out proposals to harness the two big forks of the Kings River into a series of dams, tunnels, and power plants. Some of the proposed reservoirs would be in the highest reaches of the river's canyons. Implied in all this was an extensive supporting system of roads or perhaps even railroads.[15]

After several years of intense interagency warfare, the Forest Service struck a deal with the Park Service in 1926 and allowed the limited expansion of Sequoia National Park. The enlarged park contained three times the acreage that had been set aside in 1890 but did not include any of the Kings River country. Mather's agency had to satisfy itself with taking control of the Mount Whitney region and the great glacial canyon of the Kern River. Power studies continued in the Kings River watershed, and in 1930 the Federal Power Commission issued a report summarizing the region's potential. The commission concluded that enormous amounts of power could be generated, but at considerable initial expense, owing to the region's difficult and remote terrain.

The war over the fate of the region gained a new twist after Franklin Roosevelt assumed the presidency in 1933. Far more sympathetic to preservationist views than his immediate, Republican predecessors, FDR appointed Harold Ickes as his secretary of the interior. Ickes, a Bull Moose Republican from Chicago who had fallen in with the Sierra Club, took it upon himself to push hard for a Kings Canyon National Park under the control of the Interior Department and the National Park Service. Once it made up its mind, the Sierra Club fought hard, too, with figures such as Little Joe Le Conte, now a senior member of the club's board of directors, and a young, idealistic photographer named Ansel Adams investing much time in the effort.[16] The Forest Service enlisted the help of those who hoped eventually to receive water or power from the region's proposed development. Finally, in 1940, Ickes succeeded in getting the Kings Canyon park bill through Congress and onto the president's desk. It had been a close fight, and the bill passed only after much acrimonious debate. FDR signed the legislation on March 4, 1940.

Two-thirds of a century later, Armando and I lower our packs and take a break at the summit of Pinchot Pass. Historical irony shadows the scene. The pass and peak named for America's foremost proponent of developing public lands for utilitarian purposes are now deep within national park wilderness. Pinchot would think it all a waste. He would ask why the land was set aside for so limited a use when it could do so much more. Muir, Le Conte, and Mather would revel in the wildness of Kings Canyon National Park and point out its immense symbolic and recreational value. On a late August day in the first decade of the twenty-first century, those of us who have climbed to the still-wild summit of Pinchot Pass would tend to agree with the latter group, but that's why we're here.

Leaving the summit, Armando and I begin our descent from Pinchot Pass. Twenty-five years ago I worked my way down this precipitous slope in waist-deep drifts of early autumn snow. Today, T-shirt weather reigns. Two miles south of the pass, at an altitude of about 11,200 feet, the first stunted whitebark pines appear. From the summit, we spied a cluster of small tarns in this area, and now we leave the trail and make for them. We stumble upon a narrow isthmus separating two small ponds. There we find, tucked among a copse of whitebark, an old campsite with views in all directions and settle in.

Later in the afternoon, chores done, I wander about a bit, enjoying the quiet grandeur of the setting. On the way into this campsite I had noticed a lot of fresh horse prints. Obviously, pack stock had grazed this basin within the past few days. Soon, I find the packer's camp, located behind an outcrop of granite not far from our own tents. Half buried under a pile of small stones are the remains of the packer's illegal fire, the ashes and charcoal still fresh. Why is it, I wonder, that those who travel in the wilderness with the most comforts sometimes have so different a view of acceptable impact?

The average Sierra pack-stock party travels with 150 pounds of baggage per person. I am hiking with only fifty pounds of food and equipment, yet I will honor the no-fire rule tonight. The rule, which applies to all of Kings Canyon National Park above ten thousand feet, forbids fires in order to limit the human impact on the park's sparse subalpine forests. The weather has been mild recently, so no emergency occurred here that required a fire. It appears that a packer simply lit a fire because he wanted to have one. A charred whitebark stump two feet in diameter protrudes from the rocks that half-hide the fire's remains.

In my years as a Park Service manager in the Sierra Nevada, no other wilderness issue generated as much controversy as high-country stock use. The impacts of stock users enraged many Sierra hikers who complained about meadows grazed down to stubble, trails churned to loose rubble and dust, and camps littered with manure. Stock users had an equal litany of complaints. Backpackers were rude, they asserted, and didn't understand the stock traditions of the Sierra. Worse, as the packers saw it, the managing federal agencies supported an endless assault on the traditional freedoms of the back-country, placing more limits each year on pack-stock activities such as grazing and camping.

As I noted earlier, the war continues today between these two tribes. Each has generated a lobbying group to advance its interests. Whenever Park Service or Forest Service managers contemplate a decision of any significance about wilderness management in the Sierra, the agencies expect to hear from both the Backcountry Horsemen of America and the High Sierra Hikers Association. To influence management decisions, the two sides usually resort to different strategies. During the George W. Bush era, while the stock lobby used its political connections in the Republican Party, the hikers pursued a strategy that employed lawsuits and court decisions.

In a lawsuit with major consequences for the High Sierra, the High Sierra Hikers Association, in concert with several other environmental groups, challenged the manner in which the Forest Service managed commercial stock use in the Ansel Adams and John Muir Wilderness Areas. The suit, which was filed in April of 2000, proceeded slowly, but step-by-step the Hikers Association forced the Forest Service to reconsider its relationship with the commercial pack operators who use these areas. Specific issues being litigated included party size, grazing of natural forage, special campfire privileges in otherwise closed areas, and much more. The fundamental question before the courts was whether commercial stock users deserved the right to operate in a traditional way regardless of environmental impacts.[17]

By nature, I'm a hiker and not a horseman, but my national park work connected me regularly with the world of pack stock, a useful exposure to another world that taught me much. I never learned to be a comfortable long-distance rider. I missed the flexibility of being able to stop and look at things up close whenever I wanted. I nevertheless learned to enjoy much about pack-trip life. The wilderness pleasure of a steak broiled over an open fire and a beer seduced me as easily as the next guy. Over time, moreover, I learned several important lessons. Foremost I learned that pack-stock travel involved a distinctive and very traditional culture, a culture that grew out of a deep and abiding appreciation of the freedom of being in the wilderness and of the beauty of the country.[18] The related definition of beauty, however, focused mostly on the grand scenic views and generally not on foreground details. Issues such as manure, grazing impacts, and trail damage simply did not matter to many packers. I also learned that, although the percentage of stockmen who misbehave probably does not differ significantly from the percentage of backpackers who ignore the rules, stockmen have more and bigger tools. When packers make bad decisions, their impact is magnified by their tools and their animals. A high-country camp thrashed by misbehaving stockmen in a few days may take decades to recover.

I study the half-hidden remains of the packer's recent camp. Like me, he left the trail to seek a more private camp. I find it hard not to think that he sought privacy so that he could ignore the laws that help protect this fragile timberline world. I am angered by the ultimate contradiction that plagues many stockmen: the belief that they are entitled to abuse the world they so obviously love because their predecessors were able to do what they wanted. I give credit to the hikers in at least one respect. Over my four decades of hiking in the Sierra, the community of backpackers has generally accepted the fact that changing circumstances require that wilderness use must evolve. Most hikers have learned to accept trail quotas, carry bear canisters, and even pay fees. Only a few claim the right to do what they please in the wilderness because their fathers could do so decades ago.

The Wilderness Act of 1964 committed the nation to preserving wilderness as a place to perpetuate pioneer skills. The act instructs managers to manage land in a way that will continue to facilitate "a primitive and unconfined type of recreation." Central to this issue is the question of recreational stock use. The framers of the 1964 act clearly believed that horses and mules had a place in designated wilderness. Most wilderness managers remain comfortable with this concept today. Certainly, few other forms of wilderness use can match pack stock as a way of experiencing America's historical relationship with unsettled lands. Barely a century ago, we were a society of horsemen and -women, and visiting wilderness meant using stock.

Much has changed since then, however. Changes in our culture have marginalized stock use into just another recreational lifestyle. At the same time, we have come to understand far more completely the biological impacts of stock and stock grazing in wilderness. Much of what we know about such things had not yet become apparent when Congress passed the Wilderness Act. In addition, wilderness use in places like the Sierra Nevada has shifted over time from being overwhelmingly stock-based to exactly the opposite. In the 1950s, nearly 75 percent of backcountry use was stock supported; now the figure has dropped to barely 5 percent. Under such conditions, and with many backpackers highly sensitized to the negative impacts of pack stock on trails and meadows, what future do wilderness stock users face?

I, for one, have no wish to see stock disappear from the High Sierra. In this era of high-tech, ultralight backpacking, traveling by stock, more than any other means of backcountry travel, preserves the goals of the Wilderness Act. Anyone who has wrestled with mules in the wilderness knows something of primitive recreation. At the same time, if it is to survive as a valid means of recreation in a Sierra suffering increasing biological degradation, stock-based recreation must evolve. Grazing of wild forage must end in the Sierra Nevada, as it already has in many other western wildernesses, and trails open to stock must be engineered and maintained to sustain both stock use and hiking. Trails that do not meet such standards should be closed to stock use. Critically, pack-stock users must accept that they must change. Just as most backpackers have come, sometimes reluctantly, to accept trail quotas, food storage regulations, and campfire restrictions, so must stock users. It is possible to imagine a form of stock use in the Sierra compatible with the needs of the twenty-first century, but it will not be the old way of doing things.

. . .

I'm still thinking about stock the next morning. Armando and I pass the prenoon hours descending the North Fork of Woods Creek. The descent is relentless—more than half a vertical mile downward as the morning progresses. The condition of the trail emphasizes that, unlike most sections of the Muir Trail that we've passed over in recent days, this piece has had relatively heavy stock use. The trail, built in sandy glacial soils, is loose to the point of being treacherous. The combination of loose gravel and bedrock produces a ball-bearing effect that soon makes me even more cautious than usual. I slip repeatedly and crash to the ground at least once, not a pleasant experience with a fifty-pound pack. The previous day, on Pinchot Pass, I encountered a government pack string with two mounted packers and ten mules loaded with supplies for a trail crew working in the Bench Lake area. Past experience tells me that a large trail crew requires resupply every week with the fresh food that keeps young bodies moving rocks. If this is true, this section of trail may have seen half a dozen round-trips by the supply train so far this summer, each of the passages marked by a churning of the trail surface by forty-eight iron-shod feet supporting animals weighing a thousand pounds each.

As I slide down the chewed-up trail, it occurs to me that I have stumbled into yet another ongoing wilderness controversy. The Wilderness Act of 1964, the law that created the legal concept of designated wilderness, provides federal wilderness managers with a number of basic instructions. Reflecting the philosophical nature of the statute as a whole, these instructions take the form of broad conceptual goals. Perhaps the most problematic of the Wilderness Act's precepts are the concepts of "minimum requirement" and "minimum tool." The idea is that wilderness activity by managers should be limited to that absolutely required to administer the area (the "minimum requirement"), and that the actions undertaken should be carried out using the simplest, least intrusive implements ("minimum tool"). Simple as these concepts appear to be, applying them on the ground has provided a basis for much debate.

In the Sierra Nevada, the Forest Service and Park Service have responded to these legislative mandates in different ways. For decades in the John Muir Wilderness and elsewhere in the Sierra, the Forest Service's management program has been driven by a stringent definition of "minimum tool." In a case where the means truly are the end, Forest Service trail crews work almost entirely with hand tools, eschewing chain saws and other powered devices. The Park Service, however, never content to follow the lead of its sister agency, focuses its management more on the concept of minimum requirement. Especially in the Sequoia–Kings Canyon Wilderness, the agency-defined minimum requirement for wilderness management obliges the agency to sustain a well-maintained trail system for visitor use and provide a management presence in the form of a network of backcountry rangers. "Minimum tool" thus becomes what is necessary to sustain the minimum requirement. If the trails are to be maintained, for example, and funds are limited (which they always are), then the Park Service sees the use of power tools as justified to meet the goal of keeping the trails in good condition.

The biggest debates among wilderness managers are provoked by helicopters. Few individuals in either agency oppose the use of these noisy machines to fight wildfires or carry out rescues, but wilderness purists find it hard to accept helicopters as the "minimum tool" required to support trail crews or supply backcountry rangers.

On the ground, the differing impacts of the two approaches to wilderness management are clear. As I have seen on my hike, the Forest Service staff presence in the Sierra wildernesses is faint. I walked from Yosemite to Kings Canyon on the busiest long-distance trail in the Sierra Nevada, during the busiest month of the hiking season, without meeting a single Forest Service employee. The closest I came to seeing trail work going on was a cache of hand tools behind some trailside rocks. I found the Forest Service section of the Muir Trail decently maintained, but as most Sierra hikers know, the Forest Service has little money or time to spend on secondary trails. Formerly well-engineered routes now wind around countless fallen logs and climb over rock piles.

Since entering Kings Canyon National Park, on the other hand, I've witnessed the results of the Park Service's minimum-requirement approach. I've met several trail crews working with power tools and checked in at three ranger stations. To support all this activity, the Park Service uses pack trains *and* helicopters. Choosing between the two involves the consideration of a variety of factors, including availability of stock, seasonal trail conditions, the nature of the load, and cost. To supply the work near Bench Lake, the NPS has decided to take the traditional approach and use pack stock, running a weekly pack train to the site over Pinchot Pass. This approach conforms closely to the Wilderness Act's emphasis on using primitive tools, but as I descend the trail that follows the North Fork of Woods Creek I find myself chafing against the resulting impact. My reasons have little to do with philosophy. The Woods Creek trail is ankle deep in loose gravel, and, with my heavy pack, this makes the going difficult.

I know I should appreciate this commitment to preserving wilderness character, but like most hikers, I appreciate the condition of the trail more than I dislike brief surges of overhead noise.

About noon, Armando and I arrive at Woods Creek Crossing. Here, at the confluence of the creek's two major forks, the Park Service has erected what must be the longest trail bridge in the southern Sierra. We cross the fragile-looking structure, moving carefully as the flexible span shifts under our weight. At the south end, we settle down for lunch in the shade of a massive juniper tree. An extensive camping area surrounds us, picked clean of every branch and twig by campers seeking firewood. The ground is as smooth and clear as the Astroturf in the middle of a football stadium. The big camping ground here, heavily used, confirms that our route has now merged with the Rae Lakes Loop, an extremely popular, thirty-seven-mile-long route that begins and ends at the Roads End Trailhead fifteen miles to the west. For the first time since we entered Kings Canyon National Park a week ago, good trails lead to the west, providing relatively easy access to hikers.

In the middle of this battered piece of wilderness stands a brown-painted steel box the size of an old-fashioned steamer trunk. I'm looking at what the government calls a "food storage locker." Most hikers call them "bear boxes." Originally designed for use in front-country automobile campgrounds, these containers are intended to store food in a manner that makes it inaccessible to camp-raiding black bears. After more than two decades of bear box presence in the Sequoia–Kings Canyon Wilderness, the tide has begun to turn against these improvements. The negative impact of bear boxes on campsites can no longer be doubted. At the same time, continued improvement has produced lighter and stronger individual canisters

Are bear boxes justified as a part of the "minimum requirement" for managing the wilderness? Now that good canisters exist, are boxes an appropriate "minimum tool?" The argument continues. No other Sierra wilderness provides on-site food storage containers, and their future in the two southern national parks is under review. It seems likely that the NPS will eventually phase out the boxes in Sequoia and Kings Canyon. In the meantime, camping grounds like the battered ones at Woods Creek continue to suffer from concentrated camping and the resulting impact.

As we move up the South Fork of Woods Creek, we catch glimpses of big peaks on both sides of our route. To our left, Acrodeetes Peak rises some four thousand feet above the crossing; on our right Mount Clarence King is only two hundred feet lower. We play hide and seek with both summits, watching them come into view and disappear again as we make our way past the numerous promontories and avalanche chutes that sculpt these peaks' lower slopes.

The trail, which has received no significant stock use this summer, is in good condition, and the walking relatively easy. As we move slowly upward we are overtaken by a fast-moving group of hikers. Three men in their early twenties fly by us. I ask if they are headed for Rae Lakes. "No," one of them answers as they pull away, "we need to get over Glen Pass this afternoon so that we can make it to Whitney day after tomorrow." As they disappear up the trail, I consider that Whitney is nearly sixty miles away. What do they see, I wonder, when they move through this country so rapidly?

Eventually, we arrive at Dollar Lake, the lowest of the several dozen glacial lakes that occupy the spectacular headwaters of the South Fork of Woods Creek. We begin scouting for a campsite, but before we make much progress in that quest, a familiar figure in a

gray shirt and forest-green shorts comes strolling down the trail carrying a shovel. I greet Dario Malengo, another of Kings Canyon's
veteran backcountry rangers. I ask him why he's not at Bench Lake,
his assigned station, and he shares the news that he's been called
south to free up the regular Rae Lakes ranger to help with a major
search for a missing hiker that is under way in the southernmost part
of Kings Canyon National Park. "Come on up to the station in the
morning," he says, "and I'll tell you all about it." He promises coffee,
and we guarantee a visit. We leave him to his work, which involves
inserting a displaced trail sign back into the rocky ground.

Later, over dinner, Armando and I return to the question of the
rushing hikers who passed us on the trail. Their fixation with the
Muir Trail as a physical challenge clarifies an idea that has been circling in my mind for weeks. Before I started this trip, I sought out
and reread major sections of the proceedings of the biennial wilderness conferences that the Sierra Club sponsored between 1949 and
1964. Within the four resulting volumes, one can find the words that
defined the modern wilderness movement.

As I read, it struck me that the wilderness movement dates back
to an earlier and simpler time in the Sierra. When the first wilderness conference occurred in San Francisco in April 1949, stock use
dominated the Sierra, backpackers (still known then as "knapsack-
ers") were experimenting with war-surplus plywood pack boards to
support their canvas bags, and such innovations as portable radios
and helicopters had yet to have any significant impact on the High
Sierra.

More interesting still was the pervading belief during those years
that wilderness existed for more than just recreational purposes.
As wilderness was defined in the early 1950s, its justification rested
firmly on nonrecreational foundations. Wilderness advocates such

as Howard Zahniser of the Wilderness Society, David Brower of the Sierra Club, and historian and novelist Wallace Stegner based their arguments for wilderness on two fundamental premises. First, they defined setting aside wilderness as a form of respect for the earth. We should set aside wilderness, they argued, because the world of nature deserves space where it can endure beyond our immediate influence. Their second premise defined the value of wilderness to humankind. In essence, the argument was Muir's: we need wilderness to exist so that modern, urban humans can find escape, beauty, and peace. As Stegner put it in 1959, a key purpose of wilderness is to give "a spiritual refuge to people harried and driven by the civilization men have created."[19] Later in the same essay, he rose to yet greater rhetorical heights: The purpose of wilderness, he wrote, is to give us "some humble notion of what it is to be a man, an evolved mammal, part of the natural world."

These thoughts have been on my mind because they seem to have less and less to do with what I see on the trail. Over nearly three weeks, as I have hiked south from Yosemite, I have encountered hundreds of people pursuing wilderness experiences. Some, undoubtedly, still seek Stegner's "spiritual refuge," but for many, wilderness travel has taken on an entirely new and different justification.

Throughout my hike I have both admired and worried about the superlight style of backpacking that is now the rage. No one can fault traveling light. John Muir famously explored this country in the 1870s with little more than a blanket, some dry bread and tea, and a few matches. It is not traveling light that is the issue, but rather why one decides to travel light and how ones does it. For many, the purpose is to facilitate quick long-distance travel. Day after day, as I have hiked south, I have been passed by people I've never seen again because they moved so fast. In short and hurried conversations, they shared their goals. Mostly they wanted to test themselves physically. Many hikers seek to travel between twenty and thirty miles each day, in essence turning the Muir Trail into a sequence of daily marathons. Some even run the trail.

I remind myself that moving fast in the wilderness has a long and well-documented history. Muir covered ground at a sometimes alarming pace, as did Bob Marshall, the founder of the modern wilderness movement.[20] Certainly, as they traveled rapidly, Muir and Marshall both saw a great deal and thought about what they were seeing, but how many of the superlight hikers who fly by me are engaged in the landscape and its significance? My short conversations with them leave me concerned. Many have nothing to share except geographical goals, physical accomplishment, and reports on their expensive and highly specialized equipment. I hear little in most of their conversations that captures the mid-twentieth-century view that wilderness is a place for contemplation and connection with nature.

I suspect that those who go into the wilderness primarily for physical challenge find much in the Wilderness Act arcane or even silly. Why put so much energy into cutting fallen trees by hand or worry about supplying trail crews by helicopter? If the purpose of the Muir Trail is primarily to provide a physical challenge for those who want to travel along it as rapidly as possible, perhaps the trail itself is what counts and not the country that surrounds it.

.   .   .

We visit Dario the next morning. We find him, coffee mug in hand, on the stoop of his station. Unprepossessing by any standard, the Rae Lakes station consists of a wood-framed tent cabin. A green tarp tops the rough, brown-stained single-board walls. Inside, the tiny single room, barely ten feet square, contains a built-in bunk, a table, and a wood-burning range. Packs, climbing ropes, and a fire extinguisher hang from nails. Maps fill the open wall space.

In his decades as a wilderness ranger, Dario has worked at one time or another in most of the wilderness stations in Sequoia and Kings Canyon National Parks. This summer, he's assigned to Bench Lake, but as he told us the previous night, he has come south to free up this summer's regular Rae Lakes ranger, another backcountry veteran, for temporary search duty farther south. A solo hiker with a predilection for wandering off-trail has been reported missing, and the NPS has organized an effort to locate him.

Searches both major and minor punctuate the life of wilderness rangers. In an average summer, several substantial efforts must be mounted. Each is a significant logistical challenge. A search must be designed and staff moved on-site and briefed. Once the fieldwork begins, managers must not only supply the searchers but also keep track of them as they systematically wander over often-difficult and remote terrain.

All this is going on today in another part of the park, but at Rae Lakes tranquility reigns.

Dario makes a mug of coffee for Armando, and we sit in the warm morning sun. Our conversation turns to the station itself. The NPS has plans to replace it with a fully enclosed structure more than twice as large. Dario, long accustomed to the rigors of backcountry life, confesses that he is unenthused by the proposal. He has spent summers in this simple tent frame and found it adequate. Others, including the managers at park headquarters who define the parks' "minimum requirement," see the issue differently. They believe that the summer rangers at Rae Lakes need a more secure base, not just to provide shelter but also to protect expensive search-and-rescue and law-enforcement equipment.

Internal agency arguments about what constitutes "minimum requirement" and "minimum tool" in wilderness reflect the conundrums that plague national parks as a whole. The problem, as always, is how to achieve a reasonable balance between the perceived needs of park and wilderness users and the defining vision of landscapes preserved and maintained untrammeled by humankind. How good should trails be? How much disturbance must we accept to maintain them? How much ranger presence is required to protect park resources? How well sheltered must these rangers and their equipment be? In a perfect world, answering these questions would follow useful analysis, positive public input, and negotiated compromise. In the real world, those with competing interests and relatively fixed agendas fight it out. Many such battles occur within the managing agencies, where staffs of ranger-manager-wilderness theologians debate their way through long winter meetings while the backcountry sleeps beneath the snow. In my three decades with the Park Service, I attended many such convocations.

Dario's tent frame stands among lodgepole pines on a rocky bench overlooking the biggest of the Rae Lakes. By any standard the scenery here reaches postcard perfection, one of the reasons the Rae Lakes Loop is so popular during the peak hiking months of July and August. The lakes occupy a deeply incised glacial basin. To the east, barely a mile distant, thirteen-thousand-foot summits mark the crest of the Sierra. At the head of the basin, the triangular spire of the Painted Lady, its north-facing cliffs striped with metamorphic rock, provides a perfect focal point for up-canyon vistas. A narrow band of meadow, now turning golden in the early September light, traces the shores of the lake below the ranger station. The world's troubles seem far away.

Armando finishes his coffee and we say our good-byes. Before we begin the ascent to Glen Pass, however, Rae Lakes has yet more beauty to share. A narrow isthmus, in some places no more than twenty yards wide, separates the two largest lakes, and the trail employs this natural causeway to cross to the west side of the basin. In the morning light the upper lake has taken on a stunning aquamarine tinge. In its center, with all the perfection of a traditional Chinese scroll painting, a tiny island topped with several small trees rises from the still, green-tinted water.

Two trail miles and about fifteen hundred vertical feet separate Rae Lakes from Glen Pass. Barren rock dominates, broken only by occasional fragile tufts of scarlet rumex. The panorama from the pass surrounds us with serrated summits. Peaks twelve and thirteen thousand feet high define the horizon in every direction. The Spaniards who named this mountain range in the eighteenth century got it right. The rugged skyline of the Sierra Nevada clearly displays the original idea of a mountain range resembling a saw blade—a "sierra."

To the south, for the first time on this trip, we can see the Mount Brewer country and the south end of Kings Canyon National Park. I've flown over this country numerous times, mostly as a passenger on commercial aircraft, and from thirty thousand feet it is possible to see the entire park at one time. On the ground, however, Kings Canyon feels big. It's been a week since we entered the park at its northern end, and despite our hard work, at least two more days of walking separate us from its southern limits. One of the many definitions of wilderness is that it is big enough to get lost in. Kings Canyon has that feeling. In fact, as we look south to Mount Brewer, we know that somewhere in that region someone is lost, for that is where the current search is focused.[21]

By the time we leave the pass, the day has gotten away from us.

Our schedule began to slip during our leisurely morning visit with Dario, and then we tarried too long on Glen Pass enjoying the view and conversing with fellow hikers. Now we have miles to make before dusk. The trail takes us down a steep series of sandy switchbacks, then around a rocky promontory above Charlotte Lake. This part of the Sierra has only a few natural east-west crossings, and the corridor coming into view below us has been recognized since aboriginal times as the best of them. Using a network of connecting canyons, Native Americans developed a route that led from the great Yosemite-like Kings Canyon, fifteen miles to the west, up what later came to be known as Bubbs Creek, and finally over Kearsarge Pass. Anglo-Americans first crossed this route in 1858, and the California Geological Survey, the first scientific group to enter the southern Sierra, passed through here in 1864. Charlotte Lake received its name so early (before 1873) that no one today remembers who the real Charlotte was.

On a gentle, sandy saddle several miles south of Glen Pass, many stories and trails come together. Here the Muir Trail intersects the historic east-west route to Kearsarge Pass. We, too, have come to a significant junction. Armando's time in the mountains is nearly over, and the moment has come for me to take a resupply break in the civilized world. Together we turn off the Muir Trail and head east toward Kearsarge Pass and the Onion Valley Trailhead. But first we need a camp for the night, so we take the trail to Bullfrog Lake, a scenic body of water so perfectly located that its campsites were exhausted and closed more than forty years ago. We follow the trail around the north side of the lake, passing archeological sites tucked in among glacial boulders and closed camps defined by stumps of trees cut for long-ago campfires. A half-mile beyond the lake we leave the trail and find a quiet campsite among whitebark pines.

After dinner, Armando and I drift into conversation about our time together and what we have learned about the past, present, and future of wilderness.

What does it mean to the wilderness movement that modern ecologists, historians, anthropologists, and archaeologists have soundly rejected its founding assumption? Is there a place for designated wilderness in a North America that we now know was far from being a Virgin Continent when Europeans first explored its enormous expanse?

We think back over archeological sites we visited as we trekked south. Those scatters of obsidian brought home to us the stark fact that human absence from the lands that came to form these wildernesses was not a natural state but rather a tragic, biological result of the arrival of disease-bearing Europeans in North America. Our grand unpopulated wilderness areas, we admit to each other, must be seen as accidental artifacts of our own historical presence. But does this negate their value?

Like national parks, wilderness areas reflect multiple goals. As we watch the sun descend behind the mountainous western horizon, we review in our minds what the law says wilderness must achieve. The mandate resembles the national park dream, although with subtle but significant differences. Whereas those who designated national parks set out to preserve landscapes intact and unchanged forever, those who designated wildernesses aim at a somewhat softer target: to preserve the land in a state that "generally appears to have been affected primarily by the forces of nature."[22] Herein lies something significant, we agree. National park landscapes come with defined biological outcomes in mind; wilderness landscapes do not. Instead, wilderness is intended to provide experiences, a concept that is present but secondary in the legislation that created the national park system.

Can wilderness in the twenty-first century provide valid experiences even if the original assumptions about what wilderness is include colonial and racist worldviews? The answer, we agree, is yes. Our long hike has reminded us that spending recreational time in a world with only minimal human alterations provides a valuable experience even though we know that other people once occupied these landscapes.

But the realization that much of the value of wilderness is in the experiences wilderness provides brings us face-to-face with the realization that these experiences are changing, and quickly. Speaking at the Sierra Club's 1961 Wilderness Conference, Sigurd Olson eloquently summed up the perspectives of those who created the wilderness system:

> The real significance of wilderness is a cultural matter. It is far more than hunting, fishing, hiking, camping, or canoeing; it has to do with the human spirit. And what we are trying to conserve is not scenery as much as the human spirit itself.[23]

Today, while Olson's concepts still endure for many wilderness users, wilderness has accumulated new and still-evolving reasons for existing. In our entertainment-driven culture, especially among younger users, wilderness has become not so much a place to find quiet reflection as a playground for physical and mental testing. How far? How fast? How high? Does all this activity fatally compromise wilderness? Perhaps not, but it does change it.

Are younger generations of wilderness users on their way to losing their connection with the natural world? From my boomer perspective, the worry seems real. If the primary purpose of wilderness is to face physical challenge, then much of what the Wilderness Act defines as a wilderness quality becomes superfluous. The attributes that form the heart of the legislative definition of wilderness—things like the use of primitive tools, the preservation of traditional skills, and a landscape seemingly untrammeled by humans—lose their significance. None are essential to someone seeking to set a John Muir Trail time record.

New ideas about the purpose of wilderness reflect not only our endlessly evolving culture but also the inexorable march of generational change. No generation, of course, adheres universally to a single point of view. Certainly, some ultralight hikers relate to the wilderness in the ways Brower and Zahniser intended two generations ago. But generational patterns do exist, and boomers are more likely than their children to endorse the mid-twentieth-century view of wilderness.

The shadow of the postwar generation stretches across the wilderness in other ways as well. Although the boomer generation has proven that wilderness use need not be primarily a young person's endeavor, as this generation enters its senior years it is unlikely to sustain current use levels. Within the next decade, a significant number of those now using wilderness will run up against the challenges of aging. Among my friends, bad knees, bad ankles, and numerous other ailments have begun to take their collective toll. Twenty years from now, few of us will be left to populate wilderness trails.

All of this has implications for the future of designated wilderness and how it is managed. Wilderness use in the Sierra Nevada has been statistically flat for decades, and as the boomers fade, who will replace them? Succeeding generations are smaller in overall numbers and have never engaged in wilderness recreation as enthusiastically as did the boomer parents and their parents. One can argue that less use of wilderness will not harm the lands in question. After all, these are places where the hand of man should remain light. This point is true as far as it goes, but it misses a key factor. To survive in a democracy, wilderness will continue to require an informed corps of citizens who care.

Many wilderness managers still come from the postwar generation, and their concerns reflect their generational affiliation. Park superintendents, national forest supervisors, wilderness coordinators, and wilderness rangers all worry about preserving traditional wilderness character. But while they argue endlessly about where it is appropriate to use power tools and whether helicopters can properly be used to support construction projects, it's hard not to conclude that wilderness use is likely to decline, and that wildernesses are likely to fall into the hands of generations who hold very different visions of what is important about wilderness.

Twenty-first-century wilderness will differ significantly from that envisioned in the middle years of the twentieth century. So much has changed. We set aside wilderness to provide opportunities for solitude, but modern communication devices have destroyed the isolation that wilderness once provided. Hikers now carry satellite phones, and backcountry rangers spend their evenings communicating via email on their satellite-connected laptop computers. We created wilderness to preserve traditional skills, but an overwhelming majority of wilderness users today employ the latest and newest technologies. For a few, wilderness remains the realm of ax, pack mule, and bedroll, but for most it is the land of ultralight packs, high-tech cookware, and GPS units. We created wilderness to preserve our character as a pioneer nation, but today many younger wilderness users come to wilderness seeking primarily a recreational playground for aerobic sports.

Wilderness management will have to change. For wilderness to survive as a useful concept in the coming decades, it must be adapted sufficiently to attract and hold significant numbers of new recreational users. Those who care about the traditional definitions of wilderness—and I count myself among them—need to refocus. We must learn to worry far less about matters like chain saws and helicopters and focus instead on educating potential wilderness users about why designated wilderness was created in the first place. We must reinvigorate the perception that wilderness is an antidote to contemporary urban culture. We must market this perspective because other points of view are sold daily to all who will listen. If we fail, the critical mass of political support that has created and sustained these places could easily be lost.

The competition of ideas that forms the heart of our political culture will determine the fate of our wilderness lands. Will this powerful but unforgiving forum find continuing value in this mid-twentieth-century concept? Only time will tell.

By 10:00 the next morning we're on top of Kearsarge Pass. At 11,800 feet, this is the easiest crossing of the Sierra crest within a week's walk north or south. As we descend from the pass eastward into the Inyo National Forest, we realize that it is the first Saturday in September, the opening day of the Labor Day weekend. Over the next several miles, we meet a steady stream of uphill trail traffic. A few people look like serious wilderness travelers headed in for week-long trips, but most seem to be out for shorter walks and look less well prepared. We are no longer in the world of buff long-distance hikers. This crowd is younger and more diverse than the typical Muir Trail through-hikers. We meet fat hikers, hikers with children, hikers with skin that is not white. The message cannot be ignored. For all our worrying, Americans still come to the wilderness seeking something of value.

Far below, a parking lot full of shining metal comes into view.

Distant at first, it gets closer with each switchback. I scan for a familiar car, but see nothing I recognize. About 2 P.M. I roll down the last few hundred yards of trail and approach the asphalt. As I do, my wife drives up, having just traveled six hours around the south end of the range from our western Sierra home. She sees us, waves, and finds a parking place. Happy hugs follow, and she pulls out three beers.

THREE

Sequoia National Park

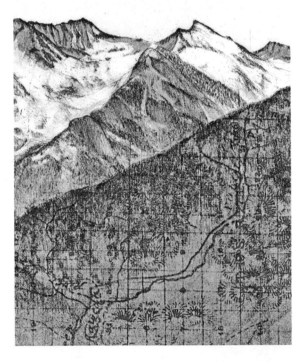

Artwork by Matthew J. Rangel, from *a transect—due east*

Monday morning—Labor Day—and I'm climbing back toward Kearsarge Pass on the same trail I walked out on just thirty-six hours ago. I'm alone once again. Armando has returned to his other life, and my short stay in civilization has come to an end. Ahead of me stretches eighty miles of trail through the backcountry heart of Sequoia National Park. I enjoyed walking with Armando for ten days, but now I'm ready to spend some time by myself. I have a lot to think about, many questions about this world of national parks yet to resolve.

As I climb the five miles of well-engineered trail to the pass, I meet many of the same people I saw hiking into the wilderness as I came out two days ago. They look different now, dirty and tired but also more composed and relaxed. The rushed desperation of Saturday has largely evaporated, leaving them seemingly more at peace with the world and each other. I say hello to those who look familiar, and several recognize me and ask where I'm headed. Reactions range from pleasant envy to exhausted disbelief when I tell them of my plans. In my mind I compare these folks to the holiday crowds in Bishop, where I just spent the weekend.

By most standards, Bishop is a small town. Only a few thousand persons call it home, yet on a Labor Day weekend the place swarms with humanity. Weekend vacationers wait in line at the town's restaurants, and those without reservations circle among the community's several dozen motels, looking for a vacancy. Highway 395 passes through the heart of Bishop's small downtown, and RVs, pickups with trailers, and automobiles back up from block to block waiting to pass through the town's several traffic lights. The congestion at times approaches gridlock, which at least makes it easier to cross the main street on foot.

After turning Armando over to friends who would take him home, my wife, Frances, and I spent the weekend in a small bed-and-breakfast within easy walking distance of Bishop's compact city center. For two nights we lived in what seemed like indulgent comfort after three weeks in the backcountry—soft beds, unlimited hot water, breakfast eggs and sausage served on china. Frances helped me with my supply and equipment chores. We visited the coin laundry, recharged camera batteries, and shopped for supplies. I worked through the provisions she brought from home and sorted out supplies for the next leg of the trip.

Mainly, however, we watched people. After three weeks in the wilderness, I was fascinated by the dense holiday population of Bishop. The sidewalks and stores seethed with humanity, and the streets remained jammed with creeping vehicles, all of them with their air conditioners running full blast. In the afternoon, our chores largely done, Frances and I wandered into the city park, where a craft fair with dozens of booths had attracted a crowd. We watched weekend vacationers shop for necessities like three-story birdhouses, chain-saw-carved yard bears, and mirrors set in old window frames. As they shopped, many munched on kettle corn and funnel cake.

As a nation, we love to vacation in the great outdoors, which is what brings so many to Bishop and the eastern Sierra, but once we've had our fill of what one recent historian has called "windshield wilderness,"[1] most are eager to return to the familiar world of shopping and snacks. The numerical drop-off between the visitor population in Bishop and that in the High Sierra is daunting for those who believe that wilderness is essential to American culture. During my town day, I shared Bishop with thousands of fellow vacationers. Indeed, on the Sunday of a three-day, late-summer weekend, the small town probably held more tourists than residents. Over the same weekend, only a few hundred hikers occupied the hundreds of square miles that constitute Kings Canyon National Park's wilderness.

Unfortunately, all this makes perfect sense. The average American child is exposed to countless television advertisements touting the pleasures of buying things. During the same formative years, that child's exposure to the outdoors and environmental education is severely limited. As a culture we have agreed that these latter things are relatively unimportant and much too expensive to be more than minor sideshows in our educational system. We are raised and educated to consume commercial products and services, and consume we do. Why sweat your way up the trail when you can tour the eastern Sierra in the comfort of your three-ton family SUV?

But now it's Monday morning, and I am sweating my way back up the trail to Kearsarge Pass and the national park boundary. Moreover, I'm enjoying it. Finally, after nearly three weeks of hiking, I'm feeling strong and comfortable on the trail. My pack is full with fresh supplies, and the uphill miles pass easily. I feel younger than I have in years.

By early afternoon, I've crossed Kearsarge Pass and reentered Kings Canyon National Park. I cautiously work my way down the steep, sandy grade that leads into the Kearsarge Lakes Basin. With my full pack I don't want to slip. Once down, I drift off the trail near the lowest of the lakes. This area receives regular peak-season use, and finding a campsite presents no problem. I find a spot I like and pass the remainder of the afternoon settling back into the rhythm of wilderness.

I'm alone. I let the quiet seep into me. I idly watch the few birds that are active on this pleasant, sunny afternoon. Juncos and white-crowned sparrows work the soil around my camp. A small flock of mountain bluebirds, their pale blue breasts the color of the sky, pay me a short visit. Across the narrow lake, Clark's nutcrackers, flashing black and white in the bright light, make themselves noisily visible. Ravens chortle out of sight.

After dinner, just as the light begins to fade, I'm surprised by the arrival of other campers. A man hiking with two preteen boys appears at the other end of the lake. I don't think my new neighbors are even aware that I'm here. Leaving the boys at a camp in the trees, the man walks down to the stream at the upper end of the lake, strips down, and takes a bath in my water supply. The volume of the lake should dilute his effect on my water, so I do my best to ignore his breach of wilderness manners. Wilderness is about freedom, I remind myself.

In the morning, I'm less sanguine. After I pack up, I wander down to the lake's outlet to fill my water bottle. I'm getting ready to pull out my water filter when I look at the stream. Soap bubbles rise from each riffle. That bastard last night used soap and turned the small stream into dirty wash water! Anger surges through me. I indulge myself a brief moment of righteous outrage and then remind myself that I'm not a ranger anymore. Without a badge or a radio, all I would likely accomplish by lecturing this fellow would be to get myself verbally abused or worse. It's time to let go and move on. I can get water from another stream.

A few minutes later I'm on the trail, but before I get very far I see a figure moving quickly toward me. As the hiker comes into view, I see that it is a ranger in full field uniform. Backcountry uniforms for national park rangers tend toward casual practicality, but this young man looks ready for serious business. Everything is just right—the green jeans with their permanent crease, the gray polyester shirt and gold badge, the forest-green ball cap with arrowhead insignia. He's even wearing his official green fleece jacket complete with gold nametag. I have no doubt that his gun and citation book are in his daypack.

We converse briefly. He's the ranger from Charlotte Lake, he explains, and he's on a mission. An adult male, hiking with his two sons on the Muir Trail in Sequoia National Park, harassed a female ranger there and refused to cooperate when she asked to see his wilderness permit. He had been involved there in some minor infraction of the rules and refused to accept her authority. Working alone, she backed off. Now this same party is at Kearsarge Lakes. Like the Mounties of the far north, the wilderness rangers are out this morning to get their man, and there will be backup this time, my ranger explains. While he closes in via one trail, the Rae Lakes ranger is approaching via another.

Quickly, I share the story of my neighbors last night and the likelihood that this is the party the ranger is looking for. I go on to explain where to find their camp. I feel like I have called down the wrath of God. This morning I approve of the Park Service's hands-on definition of what constitutes the "minimum requirement" for wilderness management. I'm pleased that there are government employees here to enforce basic rules.

Leaving the ranger to his work, I drift down the trail. I pause briefly at Bullfrog Lake to admire the perfection of this still, early autumn morning. September brings the best color palette of the year to these basins. The lakeside meadows are fully golden now, a color that sets off the powder blue of the morning sky and the reflecting water, as well as the somber green of the lodgepole pines on the far shore. Above the distant fringe of trees the serrated peaks of the

Kings-Kern Divide rise sharply into the clear air. Long morning shadows still clothe the peaks' western slopes. Except for a slight shimmering on the surface of the lake, nothing stirs.

I rejoin the Muir Trail and head south. My route descends to Vidette Meadow and then begins the 4,000-foot climb to Forester Pass on the Kings-Kern Divide. No other portion of the Muir Trail gave its designers and builders more trouble. If the Kings-Kern Divide were not so well hidden in the alpine recesses of the Sierra Nevada, we would recognize it as one of the great mountain features of the continent. Starting at 13,888-foot-high Junction Peak on the Sierra crest, the divide arcs west and then south. Ten peaks higher than 13,000 feet crown its glacier-sculpted heights. No natural pass breaks its granite wall.

The first recorded crossing of the Kings-Kern Divide occurred in 1864, when geologist Clarence King and packer Richard Cotter forced their way over the ridge using lariats as climbing ropes and carrying knapsacks made of blankets. King's account of the crossing and the subsequent ascent and naming of Mount Tyndall became one of the highlights of his 1872 book, *Mountaineering in the Sierra Nevada.* In 1915, when the route for the Muir Trail was initially drawn, the best available plan for crossing the Kings-Kern Divide was to avoid it altogether. That this detour involved two very-high-altitude crossings of the crest of the Sierra Nevada at Junction Pass (13,200 feet) and Shepherd Pass (12,000 feet), as well as a several-thousand-foot drop and climb between the two summits, only goes to show how daunting the trail's early engineers found the divide.

In the summer of 1929, a decade before the creation of Kings Canyon National Park, Sequoia National Forest supervisor Frank Cunningham took a staff party to the headwaters of Bubbs Creek. The goal of the group was to find a feasible trail route over the monumental barrier that at that time separated the Sequoia National Forest from the national park of the same name. After a good deal of mountaineering they settled on a small notch 13,200 feet high and located half a mile west of Junction Peak. With enough dynamite, trails could be constructed up both the north and south approaches to what they christened "Forester Pass." Work began on the trail the following summer, with the Forest Service building the northern approach and the Park Service constructing the south side. The two trails connected at the end of the 1931 construction season. Three-quarters of a century later, Forester Pass remains one of the scenic highlights of the John Muir Trail.

I heavily engineered trails like the one over Forester Pass, constructed at substantial cost, reflect yet another of the Sierra's wilderness contradictions. Few Muir Trail travelers question these trails, yet those who seek true wildness must admit that constructed trails dilute wilderness in a number of ways. If approached from a wilderness-purist point of view, trails scar the landscape, concentrate use and associated impact, and require intensive maintenance. Few Californians hold this view, however. Over the decades, our concept of wilderness has come to include these highly engineered mini-highways. To many, the concepts of wilderness and trail walking are inseparable. Certainly, a trip like the one I am taking would not be possible without trails. Over my lifetime I have come both to appreciate well-built trails and to enjoy escaping from them to visit more remote off-trail zones. When I leave the trail, a completely different experience results. While trail routes provide access to formally designated wilderness, I usually need to get well away from these routes to find the kind of country I think of as true wilderness. I know that such standards are relative, however, and that for many, just hiking on trails out of sight of their automobiles provides a powerful wilderness experience. In our highly urbanized culture, wilderness can mean many different things.

Although surrounded by huge peaks, the uppermost parts of the Bubbs Creek Canyon are open and sunny. Lodgepole pines grow where they can, but periodic avalanches keep much of the canyon floor free of timber. About three easy miles above Vidette Meadow, the old detour to Junction Pass branches off to the east. Here, the Forest Service began its Forester Pass project in 1930. Climbing steadily now, my trail follows a long traverse to a bench on the east side of the canyon. The last trees grow here, at an altitude of 11,200 feet, and the bench provides a logical base camp for a morning crossing of the pass. I locate a campsite and settle in.

I've paid only casual attention to the sky, so the thunder comes as a surprise. I quickly rework my camp. I pull out my tent fly and stake it down. A nylon cover goes over my pack, and anything that needs to stay dry goes into either pack or tent. For the next two hours I read and doze in my tiny tent while waves of hail accumulate on the ground outside. I creep out about 6 P.M. to boil my macaroni and cheese, but another wave of cold showers sends me into the cramped shelter of a stunted timberline tree while I wolf down my starchy meal. Only at dusk do the showers end. As the last western light warms the remaining clouds with a rich golden glow, the canyon below softly fades through a hundred shades of violet and mauve.

I awaken to a cold wet world. Rings of yesterday's hailstones still surround the stones that line my camp, and my tent sags damply. A mostly clear sky arcs overhead, so it's time to get moving. I don't want to get caught this afternoon on top of the exposed heights of the Kings-Kern Divide should the showers return. I walk for more than an hour before the warming rays of the sun finally catch me. I've left the trees behind now and entered the truly arctic world of the High Sierra. Every plant that lives here must deal with extreme cold, eight or nine months of snow cover each year, poor soil, and dry summer winds. Despite these seemingly overwhelming challenges, life persists. I traverse small pocket meadows of sedge. Two months ago, snow still covered them. This morning, autumn frost dusts their golden blades of foliage. Somewhere in between they found time to create tiny, wind-pollinated blossoms and produce seeds.

In the rocks I find even hardier plants. My favorite is *Eriogonum ovalifolium,* the oval-leaved buckwheat. This amazingly tough plant forms small, densely packed domes of tiny gray-green leaves. Although these hemispheric domes persist for decades (and possibly far longer), they seldom grow more than six inches high or a foot across. Emerging from this almost impenetrable mat of foliage are short fragile flower spikes topped with showy, maroon-colored flower heads. Each half-inch-wide head contains a dozen or more blossoms, and a mature plant can display fifty to a hundred such spikes. Each plant resembles a small granite boulder that has burst implausibly into bloom. On the barren slopes above twelve thousand feet, I find hundreds of these floral miracles scattered among the boulders and gravel.

I also find, finally, the Sierra's signature alpine plant—the sky pilot, *Polemonium eximium.* Dense hair protects six-inch-tall spikes of foliage from wind and cold. Blue-purple flower heads crown the stems. Sky pilot grows only on the Sierra's highest and most barren ridges. I've been watching for it ever since I left Tuolumne Meadows. In this stark world of rock, gravel, and cold, it suddenly appears along the trail. In a quarter mile I see several hundred plants. Almost nothing else grows around them.

I continue climbing. Forester Pass rises a full thousand feet higher than any of the other summits I've crossed since leaving Yosemite.

The starkness of this monumental cathedral of granite exhilarates me. Huge piles of sharp, clean granite boulders lead steeply upward to sculpted cliffs and ice-sharpened ridges. As I approach thirteen thousand feet, sprawling snowbanks still cover much of the rock, unmelted remnants of a winter that ended half a year ago in the rest of California. Silence soars over the landscape. Only my crunching footsteps and heaving lungs mar its perfection.

I come to the end of a long traverse, and the pass now stands clearly visible a few hundred feet directly above me. I begin a final set of short switchbacks. Suddenly, I realize that I am no longer alone. Above me, on the summit, I see two horsemen tightening cinches on a short pack train. Work done, they remount and begin their descent. As the horsemen approach, I step off the trail. It's clear that these are experienced mountain horsemen. Their five animals are strong and well fed and their tack immaculate. State-of-the-art bear-resistant food containers hang from the mules in place of the traditional leather packsaddle bags. We trade short greetings as they pass.

Five minutes later, I arrive at Forester Pass. I slip off my pack and take in the view. The final ascent on the north side has been over broken talus, but sheer cliffs fall away to the south. Two hundred feet below, the trail is carved into the granite. It stands out as the only horizontal line in an otherwise vertical world. Beyond the foot of the cliffs, stretching out to the south for dozens of miles, are the alpine headwaters of the Kern River, the southernmost of the Sierra Nevada's major rivers. I pull out my pocket-sized binoculars and scan the huge landscape. This is Sequoia National Park, my home base for the past forty years.

Still looking south, I realize that my view extends beyond the end of the High Sierra. I'm not there yet, but after more than three weeks on the trail, I'm approaching the southern limits of this alpine wilderness. The thought jars me. Until now this hike has stretched forward limitlessly. Now, standing on Forester Pass, I not only can see the end of the high country ahead but also can imagine every mile of trail that will lead me to my final destination. Casting a shadow over all this is the realization that I still have questions that I have yet to resolve. Even if I can imagine the physical trail that lies ahead, I sense there is still much to explore about the intellectual and philosophical context of this landscape. I still follow an uncertain path.

.   .   .

Less than a mile later, I'm standing by the trail taking a picture when I encounter the day's first hiker. He stops to see what I'm looking at, and his eye catches the weather-darkened brass plaque attached to the van-sized boulder. The simple memorial doesn't take long to read:

WHILE ENGAGED IN TRAIL
CONSTRUCTION AN ACCIDENT
AT THIS POINT RESULTED
IN THE DEATH OF
DONALD I. DOWNS
BORN SEPTEMBER 29, 1911
DIED SEPTEMBER 2, 1930
HIS FELLOW WORKERS PLACE THIS TABLET
TO HIS MEMORY

"This must be new," opines my companion. "I've been by here ten times, and it wasn't here before." It takes me a moment to reply. I first saw this plaque decades ago, and I know its history. I plunge in and gently offer the information that I believe that the plaque was erected shortly after the accident, and that I first saw it myself a full thirty years ago.

My new acquaintance expresses open incredulity.

The wiry, sixty-plus figure standing before me shares his credentials. He introduces himself as Reinhold Metzger and tells me that he has not only completed the Muir Trail ten times but also holds the time record for making the journey without support or resupply. His current best time for all 212 miles is five days, seven hours, and forty-five minutes. Now, he's out to break that record.[2]

Metzger travels light, carrying only a small knapsack filled mostly, I suspect, with food. To travel forty miles every twenty-four hours, he needs to move almost continuously, so he hikes when the moon is brightest. I've been watching the moon wax toward full the past few nights, so I know he'll have plenty of light to support moving tonight. He asks me to sign his notebook and note the date and time. Then he tells me that he needs to get going. Dressed in a yellow windbreaker and blue shorts, he moves lightly up the switchbacks. He has 190 miles of trail ahead of him. Metzger's High Sierra is the modern wilderness, a place for physical challenge.

As Metzger disappears up the trail, I return my attention to the plaque on the boulder. The world in which Donald Downs died has changed in many ways. The Park Service sent a six-man crew to the southern base of Forester Pass in late August 1930 to begin constructing this trail. The Forest Service had already begun work on the other side of the ridge, and the NPS needed to construct its section. If all went well, the two efforts would come together the following summer to open a crossing of the Kings-Kern Divide. The park crew, which had ridden horseback three days to reach the site, worked largely with hand tools. When shovels and pry bars proved inadequate, the men used explosives to shatter and move the larger rocks.

The crew had yet to climb above the lower, talus-covered part of the slope when the accident occurred. A routine warning that a charge was about to explode sent the men scurrying for cover. Following past experience, they sheltered behind the largest boulders at hand, several rocks the size of automobiles. The charge went off, and then, as one of the survivors put it later, a deep rumbling began across the slope. Before they could recognize the risk, the talus in which they had taken shelter began to move. The rocks moved barely five feet, but in that short distance several of the workers were partially buried. The most grievously injured turned out to be Donald "Buck" Downs, whose arm was pinned and crushed between two large granite boulders. In the aftermath of the accident, the less-injured members of the crew took sledgehammers to the rocks pinning Downs and broke him free. Then they carried him six hundred feet down to their camp.

It was at this point that reality as it existed in the early twentieth century set in. Four of the six men present at the site had been injured, and they were camped in an exposed locale 12,500 feet above sea level. Among them they had little medicine or medical knowledge, and their camp was several days' travel from help. The only option was to send one of the two uninjured men on foot to get help.

It took much of that night for their courier to reach the park's Crabtree Meadow Ranger Station, which had a telephone connection to the outside world. Once that call was made, the mobilization began. On the third afternoon, about seventy-two hours after the accident, a pack train with a doctor and medicines arrived at the site. A round-trip journey to the outside world that usually required six days had been done in barely three. During that time, however, Downs's condition had deteriorated badly.

The physician, working in a preantibiotic world, studied Downs's crushed arm and concluded that the infection that had already begun would kill Downs outright if his arm was not amputated. That evening, working to the hiss of a gasoline lantern, the doctor removed the arm. Downs lingered four more days before internal hemorrhages killed him. The others eventually recovered.[3]

The accident that killed Donald Downs would not even be life threatening today. Modern trail crews carry radios, and an accident like the one that felled Downs would be reported to park headquarters almost immediately. Park medics with drugs would be airborne within minutes and at the site within half an hour. Soon after, the injured party would be not only stabilized but also on his way to a hospital in Bishop or Fresno. Few who prize the isolation of wilderness lament the intrusion of modern technology to save lives. Death or permanent disfigurement do not rank high as goals for the "primitive and unconfined type of recreation" that the Wilderness Act calls for. Indeed, the act specifically suspends its management constraints when it comes to protecting human health and safety. Our search for wildness has limits when it comes to our own well-being.

Light showers drift across the barren landscape, but little rain reaches the ground. Yesterday's storm has drifted elsewhere. This country makes me feel small. Unlike the canyon-defined Kings River country to the north, the alpine headwaters of the Kern feature extensive rolling plateaus. Framed by high peaks to the east and the great canyon of the Kern River to the west, these tundra uplands impart a powerful sense of open space. Under foot, the terrain seems as much desert as high country. Stunted alpine plants cling here and there to a surface made mostly of rock and gravel. Not until one looks to the horizon, where snowy peaks ring the world, does the sense of "High Sierra" return. I like this country and have been coming back to it for decades. Many find it too spare, too desertlike, but to me that is its magic. I find the elemental simplicity exhilarating, even intoxicating—the same feelings that I experience when I return to the emptiness of Death Valley or the stark expanses of the Pinacate lava fields in Sonora, Mexico.

The sudden roar of a jet aircraft passing through the clouds above rudely shatters my reveries. This is not the distant sound of a jet airliner six or seven miles up, but the intense sound of a jet fighter maneuvering not far above my head. The abrupt onset of the almost overpowering roar startles me, but in a larger sense I am not surprised. Jet fighters have been a part of this landscape for decades. The eastern half of Sequoia National Park falls within the R-2508 Military Operations Area, a zone set aside and managed for military flight training. Aircraft from Edwards Air Force Base and Lemoore Naval Air Station regularly use the airspace and are often joined by planes from the Nellis Air Force Base, the California Air National Guard, and the Marine Corps. R-2508 is often a busy and extremely noisy place.[4]

The boundaries of R-2508 include not only the eastern half of Sequoia National Park but also portions of Kings Canyon National Park, all of Death Valley National Park, and extensive areas of the John Muir and Golden Trout wilderness areas. The resulting conflicts please no one. Many wilderness users find the jet fighters an intrusion in a land set aside to be "untrammeled by man." Horsemen on narrow trails worry about spooked animals and resulting accidents. Military officers, in response, point out the necessity of domestic training space and vigorously defend their use of the area.

Use rules for the area require that military aircraft remain a minimum of three thousand feet above ground level and three thousand feet away from peaks and ridges. In practice, maintaining such standards while flying over rugged terrain at speeds in excess of five hundred miles per hour is problematic. For years the NPS has tried to negotiate an agreement with the military in which all aircraft would remain at least eighteen thousand feet *above sea level,* but the military has resisted making a firm commitment to that standard. Low-flying jets periodically race through the area, and wilderness rangers receive training in aircraft identification so that they can radio in flagrant abuses. In recent years the NPS has taken military officers on pack trips into the area to try to sensitize them to wilderness concerns, and even one of these trips was buzzed by a jet flying within a few hundred feet of the ground. The embarrassed officers promised that it wouldn't happen again, but such promises had been made before.

Many have remarked on the obvious irony of setting aside an area with the intention of preserving it unimpaired forever for quiet, contemplative use while at the same time also designating it as a training site for noisy, high-tech weapons of war. During my years on these trails I've seen many military aircraft. I've taken photos myself of the *tops* of jets as they flew through canyons or passes below me. Now, no longer surprised, I simply wait for the noise to fade and move on down the trail.

I stroll southward, moving across the rocky tundra. As I descend toward eleven thousand feet, more vegetation begins to appear. Golden shorthair sedge gains enough of an edge to begin to color the landscape. In the distance the milewide valley of Tyndall Creek, with its thin forest of foxtail and lodgepole pine, comes into view. In truth, *forest* is too ambitious a word for these sparse woodlands. The trees here grow neither thickly nor more than forty or fifty feet tall. Even the densest of these timberline groves offer more sunshine than shade.

Tired now, but climbing again, I follow the trail up onto the

Bighorn Plateau. My route climbs above the last trees and wanders toward the broad summit of a gravel ridge. Scattered across the landscape are the snow-blasted remains of long-dead trees. Each fallen log is a work of art, its twisted grain exposed by centuries of blowing snow. Similar "ghost forests" occupy other ridges above the current tree line in the Kern headwaters. Researchers have documented that these forests prospered in warmer times before temperatures plunged in the sixteenth century. Reproduction ceased, and as the older trees died, the cold, dry climate prevented their decay. They lie here yet, reminders of another time.

Climbing above the remains of the fallen forest, I roll over the top of the broad morainal ridge. To the right of the trail, only a few hundred yards away, a shallow pond adds a touch of azure to this otherwise barren landscape. Two or three acres of water shimmer in the late afternoon light. I know exactly where I'm headed. Ten minutes later I lean my pack against a boulder that emerges from gravel a few dozen yards from the water's edge. Fringed by green sedge, the tarn reflects a perfect view of Mount Russell and Mount Whitney.

This camp has pulled me back several times over the years. Calling it stark does not do it justice. Absolute simplicity reigns: barren gravel, a shallow pond not much more than two hundred yards across, and an almost overwhelming 360 degrees of view. I allow my eyes to trace the full circle of the horizon. To the east, I inspect the Sierra crest culminating in Mount Whitney, now only a half dozen air miles away. Panning to the right, I shift my attention to Mount Hitchcock, Mount Newcomb, and Guyot Peak, then on to the peaks of the Kings-Kern Divide. Mountains surround me.

I set up my simple camp in the midst of this grand Zen garden. Each footprint in the weather-smoothed gravel feels like an insult to the perfection of the place. I have nowhere I need to go and little I have to do. I let the majestic quiet seep into me. At sunset, towering cumulous castles drift over the Kings-Kern Divide, each one afire with color. For a brief moment the western slope of Mount Whitney glows in purple light. Then the colors fade, but not before a full moon rises from behind Mount Russell.

. . .

I awake to find frost dusting my tent and pack. The full moon, having traversed the sky overnight, is about to disappear behind the western peaks. The sun comes quickly, an advantage of this high, exposed camp, and warms me as I enjoy my breakfast. I could easily sit here all day, sipping tea and watching the sun move across the sky, but this morning I will continue the great descent that began at Forester Pass. I have already dropped two thousand feet since I left the pass, a distance that has brought me only to the upper edge of the trees. Today my course will take me downward another three thousand feet into the great canyon of the Kern River.

I know this country well enough to recognize its biological logic. I can predict much of what I will see today as I descend from the timberline into the recesses of the Kern Canyon. First I will meet foxtail pines. Initially they will spread across the landscape, but as I continue downward their dominance will fade, and below 9,000 feet they will disappear completely. Lodgepole pines will begin to form forests around 10,500 feet, but then, as my descent continues, they will narrow their geographic spread until they grow only in cold, wet places. Today's route will take me down the precipitous canyon of Wallace Creek, and its steep south-facing slopes will provide sunny, dry habitat for western junipers. Below 9,000 feet, Jeffrey pines will join the junipers, and the rich vanilla aroma of these big three-needle pines will add a pleasant scent to the warm afternoon hours. On cool, shady slopes below 9,000 feet, red fir will begin to appear.

I'm thinking about the trees I will see as I descend, but these largest and most visible of plants form only the tip of the biological iceberg. Dozens of shrub species add complexity to the tree distributions, and hundreds of species of herbaceous plants augment the pattern. Small mammals align themselves with the plants on which they depend. Larger mammals and birds move between habitats seeking seasonal sustenance. Insects feed on all the above (including me), and modern science has yet to inventory all the fungi and microbes that inhabit the soils. Simple as this landscape may appear to the eye, I recognize this mountain world as a finely tuned ecosystem of enormous sophistication.

I also know that every facet of this time-perfected complexity faces profound and imminent change. The mainstream scientific community has long since concluded that human-induced climate change is both genuine and significant. Major media outlets like *Time* and *National Geographic* have made up their minds that climate change is real, and numerous organizations like big banks and insurance companies agree and are adjusting their business plans accordingly. Average temperatures in the Sierra have increased notably in recent decades, and careful monitoring has already disclosed change in natural systems. Sierra glaciers are melting; spring snowmelt occurs earlier than a generation ago; and the distributions of many plants and animals are shifting upward. A new era is beginning for all the organisms that live in the Sierra Nevada.

Recent scientific work should accelerate our concern. Data from many sources makes it clear that the earth's high-latitude and high-altitude areas are warming faster than low-altitude temperate or tropical climates. The High Sierra falls within a high-altitude "alpine

tundra" climate zone defined as having an average temperature during the warmest month of the year that does not exceed ten degrees
centigrade (fifty degrees Fahrenheit). A recent study by Henry F. Diaz
and Jon K. Eischeid documents the finding that, in recent decades,
more than 70 percent of the terrain within the western United States
that fell within this zone early in the twentieth century has now
warmed beyond the limit of ten degrees centigrade.[5] Put another way,
the environmental conditions that create and perpetuate tundra are
rapidly disappearing from the American West.

The Sierra's climate has changed in the past, of course, and those
past changes can teach us much about how the life-forms of the Sierra
respond to shifts in climate. During the last part of the Pleistocene
ice age, a huge glacial ice cap accumulated over the High Sierra. In
places the ice amassed to a depth of several thousand feet. This was
only the latest in a series of similar events over the past several million years, and according to many accounts it reached its most recent
peak roughly eighteen thousand years ago. After that, the climate
began to warm, and by twelve thousand years ago the big glaciers had
largely disappeared from the Sierra.

Between ten thousand and five thousand years ago the climate of
these mountains became so dry that the high-desert vegetation that
today dominates the Mono Basin to the east of Yosemite National
Park became common on the Sierra's west slope. Then, beginning
about five thousand years ago, precipitation increased, and what we
now call the Sierra "mixed-conifer" forest spread across much of the
range. More recently, the Sierra endured severe, prolonged drought
during the eleventh and twelfth centuries and then a period of colder,
wetter weather between the fifteenth and eighteen centuries. During
this latter period, sometimes called the "Little Ice Age," new glaciers

grew on the range's highest and coldest peaks. The glaciers that are now melting so rapidly apparently date from that time and not from the Pleistocene.

What all this means is that the Sierra is no stranger to environmental change. Indeed, the range's history of climate change provides a compelling window into the complexity of the earth's climate and into the implications of climate for life. The problems here, and there are several, come not so much from the process of change itself as from our human expectations about it. Because the lengths of many of these patterns exceed the lengths of individual human lives, we humans have a strong tendency to either miss or underappreciate the degree of change that affects our world. In fact, we seem strongly inclined to assume that natural things will not change unless we want them to.

Perhaps this is the heart of why we as a culture have had so much trouble facing the issue of climate change. Many citizens simply cannot imagine change on such a scale. Our vision of national parks reflects this cultural bias. Inherent in the national park idea is the firmly held assumption that the world is a stable place, and that if we are respectful of the natural world, the things we care about will endure indefinitely in their current forms. Unfortunately, this was not true when the parks were created, and it is even less true now.

When we created the first national parks, science had not yet taken an accurate measure of the earth's biological fragility. Now, we have learned not only that the earth's biological communities are inherently dynamic but also that our industrial lifestyle has significantly accelerated and intensified that natural dynamism. Climate change is not a theory but an inescapable reality that intensifies with every pound of coal or gallon of oil we burn.

Those who care about national parks and their future must face what is now an inescapable fact: neither climate change nor its likely impacts can be prevented. We have come too far already to squeeze this genie back into its bottle. The question before us as a society is not whether we can prevent climate change but the degree to which we can reduce the severest of its probable long-term impacts.

The implications of all this for the landscapes and living organisms of Sequoia National Park are profound. In fifty years or less, most of the alpine tundra of the Kern River headwaters will likely be gone. A warmer climate will melt the snow earlier even at the highest altitudes, and the growing season will extend by weeks or perhaps months. Logically, the tree line should be expected to shift upward, but that and many other potential changes in plant ranges will also be affected by longer and thus more intense summer drought. Perhaps tree species will prosper in higher places than they do now, or perhaps the already dry Kern River headwaters country will endure such long summer dry seasons that trees will fail to reproduce over significant acreages. The dead forests of the Bighorn Plateau tell us that change here is possible, but nothing guarantees what the results will be.

Atmospheric models forecast that, as the climate warms, the Sierra Nevada's snowpack will be severely affected by reduced precipitation, a rising winter snow line, and shorter winters. Only the highest terrain will support a significant snowpack in the future, and as a result California will lose a major portion of the capacity of its natural snowpack reservoir. Much of the water that now comes out of the mountains in late spring or summer as snowmelt will rush down canyons in the future as runoff during winter storms. To sustain our agriculture and cities, Californians will need to find new forms of water storage. We should not be surprised if this need turns into a campaign to construct new high-altitude reservoirs in the national parks of the Sierra Nevada. After all, we've already used most of the better lower-altitude reservoir sites.

More immediately at risk in a warming climate will be those creatures that have adapted to life in the highest and coldest Sierra habitats. Examples include the pika and gray-crowned rosy finch. In the Yosemite area, careful monitoring has already disclosed that pikas, small, guinea-pig-like lagomorphs that occupy subalpine and alpine talus fields, are shifting their ranges upward as the climate warms. The problem is that such a strategy will not work indefinitely. The mountains only go so high, and the preferred habitat of this small and traditionally common alpine creature is already near the top of the range. The problem for rosy finches is much the same. These gentle, one-ounce birds live year-round on the Sierra's snowfields and high rock ridges. As alpine creatures they will have nowhere left to go if the climate warms beyond a certain point. The same could be said for the sky pilots I found blooming on Forester Pass.

Whatever happens, the legislative promise that the national parks of the Sierra Nevada will remain "unimpaired" for future generations looks doubtful. The Park Service has spent ninety years defining this goal, and the agency's current edition of *Management Policies* provides guidance to both park managers and students of national park philosophy. Interpreting the 1916 National Park Service Organic Act, *Management Policies* still implies that impairment comes from specific management actions, and that it can be prevented. Impairment, according to the policies, must not be allowed unless authorized by Congress, and is otherwise prohibited. To make matters worse, the agency adheres to a broad definition of impairment that includes impacts not only to major park features identified in founding legislation but also to any resources that are key the "integrity of the park" or identified as "significant" in park planning processes. Another section makes it clear that the NPS must prevent any impact that would "diminish opportunities for current or future generations to enjoy, learn about, or be inspired by park resources or values."[6]

As I look around me, none of this idealistic language seems realistic in the twenty-first century. Climate change alone seems capable of turning the high country of Sequoia National Park into a profoundly different place. And, unfortunately, climate change is not the only problem facing this alpine realm. Humans have moved life-forms all over the planet, often with unanticipated results. Blister rust, a fungal tree disease native to Asia, now attacks and kills five-needle pines in western North America. Sequoia National Park's foxtail pines fall within that very category but so far have not been attacked. Other issues may come into play as well. In the Rocky Mountains, insects previously kept in check by intense winter cold are now assaulting high-altitude forests with devastating effect. Such a shift in the Sierra could further stress timberline forests.

Somber as they are, these thoughts help me see the wilderness backcountry of Sequoia National Park in a new light. When I first entered this region as a teenager, I perceived a tough and enduring remnant of an earlier, preindustrialized time. Now, four decades later, I see instead a fragile and damaged landscape headed toward inescapable change. Aldo Leopold, the prescient, mid-twentieth-century ecologist who anticipated so much of our modern world, understood this too. "One of the penalties of an ecological education," he wrote, "is that one lives alone in a world of wounds."[7] This morning, as I descend from the Bighorn Plateau, I sense wounds everywhere.

I arrive at Wallace Creek. Here, after more than 190 miles and twenty-six days, I come to the end of my Muir Trail journey. Only a dozen trail miles separate me from the summit of Mount Whitney, the southerly destination of most Muir Trail hikers, but Whitney is not my destination. Instead my goal is to head west from this point along the High Sierra Trail.

Although not as well known as the John Muir Trail, the High Sierra Trail is familiar to those who hike Sequoia's backcountry. Completed in 1932, the route runs east-west, connecting the park's two superlative features: the Giant Forest, home of the world's largest trees, and Mount Whitney, the highest peak in the forty-eight states. Fifty miles of trail lie ahead of me before I arrive at Crescent Meadow, among the Big Trees of the Giant Forest. I pull out my camera to record the moment. No one is around to take my picture, so I settle for a photo of my pack leaning against the trail sign. I note with regret that, unlike the signs farther north, the trail markers offer no trail names, only distances.

Starting westward down the High Sierra Trail takes me back to a July day forty years ago. I walked this very trail on the first major backpack trip I ever took, an adventure that exposed me for the first time to the astounding beauty of this country and to the freedom of wilderness. In the succeeding decades, I've changed a good deal more than the country around me. At first glance, nothing here seems much different. I know better, however, and as I start down Wallace Creek toward the Kern River, I vow to pay careful attention to the currents of change that threaten this land that I love.

The great descent into the Kern Canyon continues throughout the early afternoon. Slowly, the huge gorge comes into focus. The southernmost of the glacier-formed "yosemites" of the Sierra Nevada, the Kern Canyon displays all the classic attributes of its northern neighbors. Pleistocene glaciers widened a preexisting river canyon, leaving it with steep, rimming cliffs thousands of feet high and a wide and nearly flat floor.

In the bottom of this U-shaped gorge, the Kern River flows directly southward. This makes it unique among Sierra rivers. From its birth point high on the slopes of the Kings-Kern Divide, the river flows south for nearly seventy miles. No other river in the Sierra follows such a course, but then again, no other part of the Sierra has a dual crest with an eastern divide including Mount Whitney and the parallel western ridge of twelve-thousand-foot peaks known as the Great Western Divide. Geologists tell us that at least a part of the reason for this is a long-inactive fault line running north-south through the Kern River region. This zone of shattered rock eroded more easily over geological time than the country around it, and that resulted in the modern alignment of the Kern River. As a result of the old fault line, the Kern Canyon not only aligns north to south but also pursues a nearly straight course. To descend into this canyon is to lower oneself into a nearly straight, U-shaped trough thousands of feet deep. I spend much of the afternoon getting to the bottom of this gigantic linear trench.

Eventually I arrive at Junction Meadow, a boggy mix of lodge-pole pine, willow, and marshland along the east bank of the river. I scout for a campsite and find a small, rock-lined sand flat shaded by big Jeffrey pines. Wallace Creek tumbles over boulders a few dozen yards away. I set up camp, keeping an eye out for rattlesnakes. The sun disappears behind the western rim of the canyon before 5 P.M. Around me tower by far the biggest trees I've camped under in weeks.

·   ·   ·

The next morning, my route takes me down-canyon along the river. I meet no one on the trail. It appears that I have this grand place entirely to myself. The trail stays on the eastern bank of the river, and

every several miles I encounter another major tributary stream—
Whitney Creek, Guyot Creek, then Rock Creek. Around me tower
some of the Sierra's finest glacial cliffs, and not too far ahead is a
special treat. My anticipation builds as I knock off the last few miles
to Kern Hot Spring. The thought of a hot bath quickens my pace.

I know the spring well. Water bubbles out of the ground at 114°F
and fills a small natural pool. A rusty iron pipe connects the pool
with a concrete tub set in the ground fifteen feet away. Crudely
carved wooden plugs provide water control. All one has to do is
unplug the pipe leading from the spring and stopper the drain in the
concrete tub. Several dozen gallons of hot water spill into the tub and
accumulate. The water cools a bit as it hits the concrete, dropping to
a temperature that only just fails to damage flesh.

I strip down, hanging my dusty trail clothes on the low wooden
fence that runs around three sides of the tub, and settle into the
basin. Hot water spills in, and I relax and begin pouring it over my
head using a thoughtfully abandoned metal cup. I luxuriate in the
deepening hot water, spilling cup after cup of it over my back and
head. Both park rules and common sense forbid the use of soap, so I
leave it to the water alone to work its magic. I scrub down, then rinse
some of the dust out of my clothes. An easy hour passes.

In my ranger days I spent considerable time living in primitive
conditions. At various times I cooked and heated with firewood that
I cut myself, lived without electricity or telephones, and dealt with
places where plumbing did not exist and all water came directly from
creeks. Eventually, I concluded that, at least for me, "civilization"
could be reduced to a single attribute—hot water. With enough hot
water, I learned, most of the rest of the pleasures of modern life could
be discarded. Sitting in the tub at Kern Hot Spring does nothing to
cause me to reconsider this long-held conviction.

Finally, after much stalling, I dress and prepare to move on. I've soaked and scrubbed, then air-dried myself in the warm sunshine. I realize how completely I've adjusted to wilderness life after nearly a month on the trail. At home, I wouldn't think twice about the significance of a hot bath. Here, at the spring, an hour in a primitive concrete tub has provided sensual pleasures that beggar description. Half an hour later, as I move down the trail, the dust and sweat return. The memory lingers, however—the memory of a perfect moment of simple pleasure.

Half a mile south of the hot spring, the High Sierra Trail finally crosses the Kern River. A stout, wood-planked bridge spans the healthy stream. Even in September, wading this powerful stream would present a challenge. A huge granite boulder protrudes from the bank of the river and forces the stream to narrow. The bridge leaps from the boulder to the opposite bank in one span. Downstream from the bridge, the canyon floor turns marshy and the trail climbs into the adjoining talus. Here the trail crew has hewn a trail out of massive granite boulders. Drill holes document the difficulty of the work, as does the carefully laid trail surface of cleanly broken granite fragments.

At the south end of the rockwork, I come to the trail junction where the High Sierra Trail leaves the Kern River and begins its climb up the west wall of the canyon. Tomorrow morning I will make this ascent, but first I will spend a second night within the canyon. From past trips I remember a stock camp at Upper Funston Meadow, which is a few hundred yards downstream. As a hiker, I usually avoid such sites, but tonight I need a camp close to the trail junction, and Upper Funston will do.

I've hiked all day without seeing anyone, the first time this has happened on the entire trip. So I'm surprised when I arrive at Upper

Funston Meadow and find horses and mules grazing. I locate a camp to my liking, one with both a bear box and some useful half-log benches. Then, figuring that I should be friendly, I wander through the other camps looking for neighbors. I find them in the last site and immediately notice that things don't look quite right. Two men about my age sprawl tiredly in camp chairs. Around them on the ground, dumped carelessly, I see riding saddles, mule tack, and two loads of supplies. I seldom recall seeing such a mess in a stock camp.

I say hello, and it doesn't take long for the story to spill out. The two are out of Mineral King, a west-side trailhead some twenty miles away. Earlier today, while descending the Rattlesnake Creek trail, an old route that drops five thousand feet in ten miles, they suffered what stockmen call a "wreck." On a steep section of trail, a saddle horse lost its footing on slick rock and rolled. In the process the rider, who might rather have walked than ridden over this rough spot, came close to being crushed. A loaded mule went down, too, rolling over onto its back and on down the rocky slope. Fortunately, neither animal suffered crippling injuries, but the rider came away with bruises and cuts and an ankle that is sprained or worse. The two men repacked and resumed their journey, arriving finally at Funston Meadow. It could have been far worse. Having a horse roll over you on a rocky slope can be life-threatening.

There isn't much I can do but offer sympathy and ibuprofen. They accept the sympathy and say no thanks to my relatively weak medicine. Apparently they have better drugs than I do. I leave the injured rider to massage his wounds and return to my camp. An hour later, while I'm boiling up my evening meal, the uninjured of my two neighbors wanders into my camp and invites me over for dessert. I promise to join them once I've put things away for the night. Later, around their campfire, we trade sugar and stories. I eagerly wolf down a piece of chocolate-frosted cake that comes out of one of their food boxes. Two days on the trail and a mule wreck have done it no harm. Then we tell mountain stories.

The stockman who invited me over has been riding in these mountains since he was a small boy, a time he admits is now fifty years past. As a teenager, he worked as a pack station wrangler and led trips into these very canyons. As the campfire illuminates the darkening woods, he recalls adventures from long ago and laments current conditions in the mountains. He pulls no punches. The Park Service, he says, has ruined the backcountry for stockmen. The trails are in terrible condition and there are too many rules. All the fun has gone out of it. Eventually, the stories wind down, and I return to my camp. As I crawl into my sleeping bag, I consider the irony of it all. In this world of change, even wilderness users can feel like righteous victims.

Dawn arrives to the sound of horses. Typically, the stock have been active most of the night. Horses in the wilderness graze much more actively than those in domestic pastures. Now I hear them feeding within a few yards of where I lie. When I first camped among free-grazing stock, I used to worry they might step on me while I slept. My tent, after all, is not much higher than many of the fallen logs that surround Upper Funston Meadow. But over the years I've come to trust these gentle giants. I have never heard of a horse stepping on a sleeping human. Because of their ceaseless activity, the stock cost me some sleep, but I have no complaint. I chose to camp among them.

The sky lightens, and I slip out of my tent. I have a canyon wall to climb this morning, and I might as well get an early start. I've come to the end of the great descent that began at Forester Pass. Over the past three days I have given up over sixty-five hundred feet of altitude. Today I will have to regain much of that as I move westward toward the Great Western Divide.

Built in the early 1930s, at the same time as Forester Pass, the section of the High Sierra Trail that climbs west from the floor of the Kern Canyon displays the careful engineering that typifies many other trails of that era. The route switchbacks up a steep ravine that breaks the canyon's western wall, and the engineers who designed it worked hard to fit the trail into the difficult terrain. For the first two miles the trail maintains an almost perfect grade as it zigs and zags between the cliffs and bluffs that confine the ravine. I'm glad I started early. I can imagine the heat here on a sunny July afternoon.

For more than an hour I watch the canyon floor drop away and the view grow ever more expansive. I'm a full ten miles downstream from where I first entered the Kern Canyon, but its character remains unchanged. By the time I've climbed the first thousand feet, I can see again the full U-shaped sweep of this gigantic gorge. I've climbed up to meet the sun, and I can see its rays beginning to touch the canyon floor. Far below I spy, at Upper Funston Meadow, two horses and two mules still grazing near the camps.

A lightning fire crept through this country in the summer of 1996. Ignited by a thunderstorm in early August, the Big Arroyo Fire burned for almost three months and thinned vegetation over more than five square miles. The Park Service, pursuing its policy of natural processes, monitored the fire's progress and effects but largely allowed it to follow its own will. A decade later, my route displays a full range of fire effects. I climb through patches of lodgepole pines that suffered almost 100 percent mortality. In such places, the fire-killed skeletons of the old trees are beginning to fall, and a new generation of young pines completely clothes the ground. Lodgepole pines, in fact, have a cone and seed structure that makes them especially successful after fires. I wander through dense growths of ceanothus and gooseberry, shrubs that have taken advantage of the sunshine and nutrient availability that follows a fire. Occasionally, I find larger Jeffrey pines and red firs. Big trees like these, often three or even four feet in diameter, usually survive burns. Many of these survivors display basal fire scars on their trunks, the result of numerous past fires. On the dead lodgepoles I see woodpecker work, and I watch carefully. One of my goals on this trip, unfulfilled so far, is to see a black-backed woodpecker, a rare subalpine species, but once again this species eludes me. I do startle a young back bear, however, the first one I have seen on the entire trip. The bear is feeding on gooseberries but retreats quickly when it senses my presence.

The forest thickens, at least where the fire did not burn hot, and the terrain levels. I have reached the rim of the Chagoopa Plateau. A generous triangle covering almost ten square miles, this forested upland ranges from nine thousand to more than eleven thousand feet in height. Deep glacial canyons define two edges of the plateau, while the Kaweah Peaks Ridge, rising to more than thirteen thousand feet, provides the third boundary. Only one maintained trail, the High Sierra, accesses the plateau. All this geography combines to give the plateau an unsurpassed sense of isolation.

A quarter-mile detour from the High Sierra Trail takes me to Sky Parlor Meadow. What a perfect name! Nearly a third of a mile across, this spacious seasonal wetland rolls out before me in modest perfection. With the meadow nearly dry now that the summer is winding down, the sedges have taken on a wonderful golden glow. As I wander out into the meadow's exhilarating openness, I find thousands of royal blue gentian blossoms hiding among the sedge. To the north, clearly visible, the broad symmetrical cone of Mount Kaweah dominates the skyline. A low fringe of lodgepole defines the meadow's borders. Grand and formal in its simplicity, this is indeed a giant parlor in the sky.

For the next several miles the trail climbs northwesterly across the gently rising surface of the plateau. The Big Arroyo Fire affected much of this country. What will happen the next time this country burns, I wonder? As the climate warms in coming decades and the duration of the dry season lengthens, will this fragile, high-altitude forest survive? Already, the trees of the Chagoopa face formidable stresses in the form of intense winter cold, poor soils, and summer drought. The next round of disturbance in this forest could send it over the edge in terms of its ability to recover. This question applies to all the forests of Sequoia National Park, but the fact that this remote forest, so far from most human activity, is at risk makes a powerful point. Only a handful of the nation's fifty-plus national parks take their names directly from living species. Sequoia was the first such place and, for decades, the only national park to celebrate its biological resources in so clear a manner.[8] Now, despite legislation that protects this great natural reserve on paper, all of its biological resources are at risk.

Intensive studies of past periods of climate change in the southern Sierra suggest much of what may happen. As the climate changes, the Sierra's life zones will begin to unravel. Plant communities will not move as intact ecosystems but rather will likely disintegrate and reassemble in new ways. Each species will respond individually. Some will move to higher elevations; others will remain in place but function differently within the evolving ecosystems. Yet other organisms will disappear completely. Once the great scramble for survival begins, the forests and ecosystems we know will turn into new and sometimes unrecognizable places.

All this has happened before, of course. And we have been able to piece together much of what resulted. Many species disappeared. By the time Europeans arrived to stay in California in the late eighteenth century, the land no longer supported camels, native horses, giant sloths, and mammoths, all of which lived in California until recent geological times. The Pleistocene fossil record preserved in such places as the La Brea Tar Pits in Southern California suggests the scale of loss. Hundreds of species of animals disappeared. They ranged in scale from mice and small songbirds to huge bears and elephants. Significantly, this profound period of biological collapse coincided not only with a time of rapid climate change but also with another biological change, the arrival of human beings as active predators.

Scientists continue to debate the relative roles of climate change and human activity in the collapse of California's Pleistocene fauna, but most of these now-extinct species had successfully weathered more than a million years of oscillating climate shifts between glacial and interglacial periods until humans arrived to assume the role of top predator in the ecosystem. Similar factors seem fated to work together again.

Rapid climate change will partner with intense new human impacts. This time we humans are working not with spears but with a much greater arsenal of tools. In less than two hundred years, using everything from bulldozers to microprocessors, we have changed the landscape of California almost beyond recognition. Over large areas, which include not only urban landscapes but also extensive agricultural tracts, almost nothing remains of California's pre-nineteenth-century flora and fauna. At the same time, we have profoundly altered the region's aquatic systems, draining rivers and wetlands, and changed the nature of the atmosphere itself. Farmers within Tulare County alone (Sequoia National Park's home) annually apply more than fifteen million pounds of toxic pesticides and herbicides. The surrounding counties see even larger amounts used.[9] Much of this material volatizes and disperses as it is sprayed.

Aside from the narrow trace of the trail beneath my feet, the Chagoopa Plateau seems untouched by humanity. I've not met a single hiker today. I wrestle with the incongruity of it all. The remote country of the Chagoopa is safeguarded both by geography and by law. It takes several days to reach the plateau regardless of where one starts, and this country is set aside as both national park and as designated wilderness. I can imagine no better-shielded place. But I also know that it is not protected well enough to ensure that it will not change. I move along the trail with a mixed sense of privilege and impending loss. The forests and wildlife here remain much as they were when Europeans arrived in California two and a half centuries ago. Few places have changed less. Yet I also know that, for the existing ecosystem, time is running short. Today I have it entirely to myself. Within my lifetime, it may cease to exist.

. . .

By midafternoon I arrive at my destination, a large, unnamed meadow on the high northwestern corner of the plateau. Most wilderness travelers in this region stay overnight at Moraine Lake, a handsome body of water set in a thick lodgepole pine forest near Sky Parlor Meadow. I have no urge for human company, so I've sought out a quieter camp.

I've climbed so high today that open stands of foxtail pine grow on the sandy, rolling terrain that surrounds this meadow basin. A fringe of water-loving lodgepoles grows closer to the meadow. Mount Kaweah, almost fourteen thousand feet high, towers imposingly beyond the trees at the north end of the meadow. Amazingly, I find no regularly used campsite. I widen my search and eventually find a quiet site with the requisite level sandy spot for my tent, and flat granite kitchen rocks. The site shows no sign of previous human use, but my night here will do it little harm. I have no plans to build a fire, so I will leave little more than footprints to be erased by the coming winter.

I have this wonderful place to myself, and I savor the last hours of the afternoon. I sit for a spell on my kitchen rock, then rise and wander about absorbing the place. The meadow below my camp shimmers in the late afternoon sun, its foliage gone crisply golden. Even with the sun still shining I can tell that there will be frost tonight. This afternoon I have a strong sense of things ending. Both the summer and this trip are nearly over. For weeks I have walked toward a destination beyond the horizon, a place sufficiently distant to be beyond easy imagining. Tomorrow afternoon I will cross my final pass and begin my descent toward civilization.

I know also that, just as my summer adventure and the season of summer itself must come to an end, so too must the national park dream as we envisioned it in the twentieth century. The past few days have convinced me beyond any doubt that not even the remote heart of Sequoia National Park can escape the impacts of anthropogenic biological change. The implications of this conclusion for the national park dream is profound. I must face the realization that national parks, and to a significant degree wilderness areas as well, reflect the obsolete science and culture of the late nineteenth century. The national park idea promises that landscapes and their special features can be preserved "unimpaired" essentially forever.[10] Now I know that this is impossible. A century ago, in a time when the cumulative global effects of human activity were much smaller, this view provided useful guidance for park managers. Today, the idea that the parks can protect forever everything significant within their boundaries reflects a mind-set somewhere between denial and fantasy.

It's daunting to imagine the ecological implications that this new century has already begun to reveal, but leading this suite of threats is global climate change. The destabilizing process of climate change in the Sierra has already begun. It appears likely that this new century will witness sufficient continuing warming to mean that nearly *all* the Sierra Nevada's native plants and animals will need to relocate from their current geographical ranges. To the uninformed this may sound unlikely, but an average temperature increase of just three degrees Fahrenheit would have the effect of requiring every life-form in the Sierra to shift its range upward a full thousand feet vertically, a shift that in many cases translates to miles on the ground. Climatological data suggests that we are already approaching this dubious goal.

To make matters worse, we already know that other stresses will heighten the effects of climate-related change. Fires will intensify in both geographic spread and effect. Nonnative life-forms can be expected to invade disturbed plant communities, bringing into already-stressed ecosystems not only new plants and animals but also new insects and pathogens. There may well be strong pressure to harvest these damaged forests for human use before they are lost to the currents of change. In the past, defenders of parks and wilderness argued against utilization of these resources by pointing out the scientific, esthetic, and ethical importance of leaving them alone. But now, if science tells us that change is inevitable, all these arguments weaken.

We know now that biological change on this planet will not pass over the biological islands we have created and leave them untouched.

The engines of climate change, habitat fragmentation, and global pollution will carry out their powerful work on all landscapes. If remote places like Greenland and Antarctica cannot escape agents of transformation like climate change, how can we continue to manage the Sierra Nevada of California under the assumption that impairment of its natural resources can be effectively prevented by legislative mandate and the use of natural processes like wildland fire?

In the morning, I abandon the Chagoopa Plateau and move northwestward along the rim of the glacial gash known as the Big Arroyo. There the High Sierra Trail follows a natural bench confined on one side by the thousand-foot drop-off into the Big Arroyo and, on the other, by the massive bulk of Mount Kaweah. The bench itself alternates between rocky granite hillocks and rolling, sandy soils. Foxtail pines grow exuberantly here, or at least as exuberantly as organisms can that spend more than half their lives enduring arctic cold and snow. Here, in scattered stands with much open ground between them, individual trees achieve massive girth. Trunks six feet thick are common. Many trees have died back during hard times, and the resulting dead limbs and crowns stand golden against the sky. Here and there completely dead trees stand gloriously, wind- and snow-sculpted into abstract spires with the rich warm glow of ripe wheat fields. Ansel Adams photographed foxtails along this trail in the early 1930s, and I cannot resist doing the same. With the morning light to my back, I use the serrated peaks of the Great Western Divide as background for several tree skeleton images. Beyond those summits lie the Kaweah River country and home.

The trail begins a long, gentle, side-hill descent into the Big Arroyo. Yet another example of early-1930s engineering, the route follows an easy grade across the steep and unstable slope. Pleistocene glaciers left this mountainside covered with rocky debris, and boulders still roll regularly here. A powerful storm last winter blew down stands of thousand-year-old foxtails, ripping clusters of them out of the ground and leaving them all pointing the same direction. Now, eight months later, the last brown needles are falling off the shredded branches of these felled giants.

On the floor of the Big Arroyo I encounter human company, a Park Service wrangler leading twenty horses and mules back to a work camp. Apparently the stock wandered far afield overnight, and it has taken most of the morning to find them. The afternoon plan, he tells me, is to pack up a trail crew and move it to Upper Funston Meadow in the Kern Canyon for an end-of-the-season project.

I begin the climb to Kaweah Gap. The trail ascends into the grand, ice-scoured head of the Big Arroyo. Ever since I left the Chagoopa Plateau, the Kaweah Peaks Ridge has been angling ever closer to the Great Western Divide, and now these two massive spines of serrated peaks close in on their junction point just south of Triple Divide Peak. I move into this narrowing angle. The remote summit of 13,700-foot Black Kaweah rises assertively on my right. This huge mountain of dark metamorphic rock has a dangerous reputation among mountaineers. Its upper reaches, badly fractured by countless millennia of frosts, offer few secure handholds. Every rock seems ready to convert itself into a projectile aimed toward those still below. To my left, the granitic peaks of the Great Western Divide shine brightly in the midday sun. Although not as high as the Kaweahs, the summits of the Great Western Divide still impress me. Lippincott Mountain, Eagle Scout Peak, and Mount Stewart all rise above 12,000 feet.

Pleistocene snows accumulated so deeply here that the resulting glacier eventually overrode the crest of the Great Western Divide and cut an erosional gap westward between Eagle Scout Peak and

Mount Stewart. The High Sierra Trail seeks out this gap to continue its progress toward the Giant Forest. Ascending to Kaweah Gap, as this notch is known, is easy enough from the east. The glaciers cut the notch down to within a few hundred feet of the altitude of the Arroyo's floor. I am soon on top.

Although Kaweah Gap is one of the lowest passes of my entire trip, it lacks nothing in grandeur. Big mountains and imposing scenery surround me. Mount Stewart looms immediately to the north; to the south it is matched by the towering bulk of Eagle Scout Peak. Looking behind me, I can survey the barren headwaters of the Big Arroyo and the remote summit of Black Kaweah. To the west, where I am headed, the terrain drops off so quickly that I cannot see where the trail goes. I can see the summits of numerous ridges and peaks, however, and I recognize them instantly. Alta Peak, 11,204 feet high, can be seen from the living room of my home in the foothill town of Three Rivers.

Bolted to the bedrock beside the trail, I find yet another metal plaque. This one, also erected in the early 1930s, honors George Stewart and recognizes him as the "founder of Sequoia National Park." I know Stewart's story, and it, too, speaks of societal change. In the late 1880s, while serving as the editor of a Visalia newspaper, Stewart envisioned a national park in the Kaweah River watershed to protect the best of the giant sequoia trees. He led the successful campaign to create the park in 1890, and for decades thereafter the small farm town of Visalia, Tulare County's seat, maintained close ties with the national park its citizens had created.

More than a century later, that relationship has evolved into something less certain. Tulare County, once rural and agricultural, now has more than four hundred thousand residents, and once-tiny Visalia is the core of a federally recognized metropolitan statistical area with more than two hundred thousand residents. Traditional national park philosophy suggests that the wildlands of Sequoia National Park should gain ever-higher significance to the residents of Visalia and Tulare County as the region urbanizes. The reality is more complex. Over time the growing population of Tulare County has lost most of its once-close relationship with its national park. A majority of the county's residents make little use of the park, and many have not ever visited it, although the park's mountainous terrain can easily be seen on clear days from most of the county's cities and towns.

The elected county supervisor whose district includes the park has stated on record that the park is too restrictive and should be opened to more commercial forms of recreation. Indeed, Tulare County's board of supervisors spent hundreds of thousands of dollars pursuing a futile lawsuit intended to challenge and terminate Clinton-era protection for the sequoia groves located in the national forest that surrounds the national park. On a more positive note, Visalia's city government in recent years began to take a fresh and more positive look at its neighboring national park, although primarily with an eye to using the park and its visitors to increase commercial activity within the city.

Looking westward from Kaweah Gap brings me face-to-face with another issue that ties together town and park—air pollution. For weeks I have enjoyed vistas largely unsullied by haze or smog. At Kaweah Gap this run of good air comes abruptly to an end. To the west, a gray-brown haze smothers the landscape. Summits only a few miles distant have lost their color and sharpness. Farther west, the Sierra's foothills show only as indistinct mounds. As for the San Joaquin Valley itself, it is completely invisible, engulfed in a dense particulate haze largely of its own making.

The high peaks of the Great Western Divide rise closer to the San Joaquin Valley than any other part of the High Sierra, and this proximity bathes these grand summits in auto exhaust, dust, smoke, and farm chemicals. Sustained ozone levels in the western part of the park match or even exceed those of Los Angeles during the warm summer months. Much research has yet to be done on what all this means, but preliminary results cast a dark shadow over the landscape. West of the Great Western Divide, for example, nearly two-thirds of the park's Jeffrey pines display ozone-caused foliage damage. The fact that these trees grow between six thousand and nine thousand feet above the San Joaquin Valley floor has not spared them. The same ozone leads to advisory warnings for park hikers. On a majority of summer days, the ozone is so bad that ozone-sensitive park visitors should refrain from outdoor physical exercise. Some summer days, even at six thousand feet, park rangers must recommend against hiking among the sequoias. Those who do so risk damage to their lungs.

The environmental deterioration of the western half of Sequoia National Park has occurred despite laws that theoretically prevent such things. The National Park Service Organic Act of 1916 requires that the park be preserved "unimpaired." The Clean Air Act of 1963 and its amendments specifically address air quality protection for national park lands, but it is clear that in the twenty-first century these laws are incapable of producing the results they were intended to achieve.

Once again I face the inescapable conclusion: not only will these parklands change in the future, but also they have already changed significantly for the worse, even as most park rangers (myself long included) have continued to assure the public that the parks are being successfully preserved for posterity. Staring out across the sea of smog that smothers Central California in late summer, I know that such a promise approaches outright falsehood. I also know from personal experience, however, that park stories reflect the idealism and hope of the ranger corps. The stories are not so much conscious falsehoods as unreasoned optimism, continued belief in the park ideal pursued in denial of obvious fact.

I begin the descent from Kaweah Gap. More than thirty years have passed since I first hiked this portion of the High Sierra Trail, and its scenery still takes my breath away. The route ranks, by any standard, as one of the most scenic trails anywhere in the national park system. For sheer audacity in the face of difficult terrain, it may be unsurpassed. The construction of the High Sierra Trail up the west side of Kaweah Gap between 1930 and 1932 still stands as one of the great trail-building efforts in Sierra Nevada history. Barely a straight-line mile separates Hamilton Lake, located at the western base of Kaweah Gap, from the summit; the engineers who located the trail needed to find in that distance a way to allow the trail to climb twenty-five hundred vertical feet. They used every trick they knew, blasting the tread out of bluffs and cliffs of crystalline granite. The final design required five miles of trail to cover the air mile between Hamilton Lake and Kaweah Gap.

The trail leads down a rocky draw. Snowbanks linger from last winter. The great north wall of Eagle Scout Peak towers to my left, a huge mass of exposed granite. During colder periods, glaciers grew here, and their evidence is everywhere. Still following the draw, the trail comes to the jumbled boulders of a moraine. Angularly cut, these huge pieces of stone show little weathering. They may have been dumped here as recently as the Little Ice Age only five hundred years ago.

I follow the trail through the rocks—construction here must have been hard—and move inside the recently melted glacier's bed. Geological freshness pervades the landscape. Nowhere else on this trip has the evidence of past ice been more powerful. I round a bend in the trail and stare into Precipice Lake. Turquoise-green water fills a seemingly bottomless cleft in the rock. Vertical granite cliffs form the lake's opposite shore. Even at its widest point, this body of water is less than a hundred yards across, and the cliffs opposite tower overhead. Snow still clings to the cold, shady cliff. This perfect ninety-degree junction of rock and dark water has attracted photographers since the trail opened in 1932. Ansel Adams was among the first, and the image he made here, titled *Frozen Lake and Cliffs*, remains one of his best-known Sierra Nevada photographs. Prints hang in museums and galleries worldwide, but this afternoon I have the real thing to myself.

A narrow rim of granite separates Precipice Lake from the great void below, and I find a small rock-rimmed ledge of sand that previous hikers have laboriously cleared for sleeping. Below me, the world rolls away into a wonderland of cliffs and domes, an imposing granite complex that the Park Service long ago named Valhalla, and somehow the idea—that this is a place for gods—works.

For the last time on this trip, I set up my simple camp, savoring the familiar process. It never takes long. I unroll my tent, insert the two wands that give it structure and spike it down. Into the thirty-inch-high shelter go air mattress and sleeping bag. The kitchen doesn't take much longer. I pull out my tiny one-burner stove together with its pan and teakettle and set them up on a level piece of bedrock. Last out of the pack is my padded stadium chair. I'm home. According to my journal, this is Camp Twenty-Four.

I pass the waning hours of the day watching the play of light across the landscape. This is the country that captured me so long ago and set me on the life course I've followed since. For the past twenty years I've made my home fifteen straight-line miles down the canyons that begin here. Just looking at these ridges and canyons gives me a powerful sense of having roots. While I prepare dinner, I try to ignore the smoggy haze. I keep the camera handy in the hope that the day's final rays will add richness to this already stunning landscape, but the air to the west is so thick with pollutants that the sun disappears into the smog before it reaches the horizon. My national-park day ends not in a blaze of alpenglow but in a somber world of fading gray.

. . .

I crawl out of my tent at first light. Overnight the pollution has retreated down-canyon. Far below, Hamilton Lake and the Valhalla nestle in deep shadows. Although the upper end of Hamilton Lake lies less than half a mile from my ledge, I know that it will take me several hours of walking to make my way down the trail to the lakeshore.

The steady downgrade makes for easy hiking, so I focus on the scenery and the amazing vision of those who pushed the trail over this mountain so long ago. Alternating between switchbacks and westerly traverses, the trail makes its way downward across the cliffs that form the northern wall of Hamilton Lake's rockbound setting. Small thickets of chest-high willows appear among the rocks, and they are full of birds feeding on seeds and the last of the summer's insects. I catch glimpses of white-crowned sparrows, MacGillivray's warblers, green-tailed towhees, and lesser goldfinches. The sun spills over the ridge behind me, illuminating the nascent fall color in the willow leaves. Once again the High Sierra Trail has worked its magic on me. I can think of nowhere else I'd rather be.

About a mile and a half below Precipice Lake, I arrive at Hamilton Gorge, the greatest of all the obstacles faced here by trail builders in the early 1930s. Not a gorge in the traditional sense, but rather a nearly vertical chimney in the steep cliffs that rise above Hamilton Lake, Hamilton Gorge initially stumped the Park Service's trail builders. More than a hundred feet across and with walls rising in perfect verticality, the deep gap in the cliff face held ice and snow in its shady depths well into the summer. The service's engineers solved the problem with a literal leap of faith. In the fall of 1932, using forty thousand pounds of steel and concrete packed to the site by mules, the Park Service erected a soaring suspension bridge across the cliff face on the outer rim of the chimney. Several hundred feet of air separated the center of the span from the rocks far below. In an era when Park Service and Forest Service crews were building trails all over the Sierra, the Hamilton Gorge bridge stood unique. For sheer audacity, no other wilderness structure in the Sierra Nevada approached it.

Like many audacious structures, the Hamilton Gorge bridge had a short life. Barely five years after its completion, a powerful avalanche tore the bridge away from its concrete footings and deposited its twisted remains a thousand feet below, not far from the shores of Hamilton Lake. Determined to reopen the trail, the Park Service returned to the site and tried another solution. This time, using hundreds of pounds of explosives, the agency blasted a ledge into the recesses of the chimney and back out again. Portions of the cliff were so steep that the trail had to be cut into the rock as half-tunnels. At one point the trail tunnels completely inside the cliff—burrowing through the rock like a mining adit—and then reemerges.

This second try worked better than the first and endures today. I pass through the short tunnel, marveling at the effort that went into making this country accessible. Beyond the tunnel's exit portal, the trail meets the west end of the bridge site and the original grade. Heavy concrete footings still define where the bridge stood, and a massive roll of steel cable rests yet where it was placed after the avalanche swept the bridge away. Some hikers, I suspect, see the cable as trailside litter. To me, it speaks of history and of the power of this landscape to derail human plans.

By lunchtime I arrive at Hamilton Lake. No longer do I have the sense of being on top of the world. The lake, despite being nearly half a mile long, seems almost small in comparison to the landscape that surrounds it. Cliffs one to two thousand feet high closely encircle three sides of the lake. On the slope to the north are the switchbacks that brought me down from Precipice Lake, situated far above on its narrow ledge. The upper portions of the switchbacks show clearly against barren rock, but as my eyes follow the trail downward it enters a thick carpet of manzanita. Jeffrey pine and massive old western junipers rise here and there above this montane chaparral. Looking at those high slopes, I realize that I have left behind the High Sierra.

I consume my all-too-familiar hiker's lunch beside Hamilton Creek just below the lake. Big red firs grow here, and I enjoy their shade. An ouzel feeds on insects in the creek, and I watch a sharp-shinned hawk dive unsuccessfully after a sparrowlike junco. There are people about, too. Hamilton Lake, with its spectacular setting, is a destination for hikers. I see backpackers camped on the open bedrock near the lake's west shore and encounter some clean-looking day-hikers who have likely trekked five miles up to the lake from the Bearpaw Meadow High Sierra Camp. I'm headed to that camp myself this afternoon, and I find myself anticipating its hot showers, beds, and hearty meals.

Although not as wildly scenic as the section above Hamilton Lake, the High Sierra Trail west from the lake still offers genuine drama. The altitude at Bearpaw is only a few hundred feet short of matching that of the lake, but the settings of the two differ strongly. Unlike Hamilton Lake, which is set deeply into its glacier-scoured and cliff-rimmed basin, Bearpaw occupies a hilltop setting on the rim of a canyon. In theory, all the trail builders of the 1930s had to do to connect the two points was keep an even grade along the canyon wall. In attempting to execute this vision, however, they found themselves dealing with sheer cliffs, rolling granite domes, side canyons, and all manner of other physical obstacles.

Three-quarters of a century later, I enjoy the results of their labors. When the trail was built, pursuing a perfectly even grade proved too difficult and would have scarred the landscape too much, so the route instead moves up and down along the north wall of the canyon. Here and there, depending upon the terrain, the route rises above a particularly vertical cliff or drops to seek a bridge site. The views never falter, however. As the trail moves west, the Middle Fork of the Kaweah River drops away ever deeper into its growing canyon. As that gorge deepens, the trail stays high. Much of the route is cut from hard rock. In places the laborers of the early 1930s blasted a hard-rock ledge wide enough to allow passage of an automobile. The miles pass easily, and I walk into Bearpaw by midafternoon.

At Bearpaw, on a handful of acres excluded from designated wilderness, the NPS maintains a small settlement that it first developed in the 1930s, shortly after the completion of the High Sierra Trail. On the granite rim of River Valley—the Yosemite-like glacial canyon of the Middle Fork of the Kaweah River—hikers encounter a cluster of simple facilities. At the upper end of the camp, overlooking the trail from Hamilton Lake, is the Bearpaw Meadow Ranger Station, a 1960s A-frame that provides summer quarters for the backcountry ranger who patrols this part of Sequoia National Park. Immediately behind it stands the original ranger station, a 1930s log cabin erected by the Civilian Conservation Corps. At the lower end of the camp, travelers find the Bearpaw Meadow Campground, complete with numbered sites and piped water. In between stands the High Sierra Camp, a complex consisting of half a dozen wood-floored sleeping tents, a larger dining room/kitchen tent structure, and a handful of small support structures housing staff, showers, and even a flush toilet.

Bearpaw High Sierra Camp opened in 1934, and, aside from a few summers during the Second World War, it has operated each summer since. Predating the modern wilderness movement, it reflects a Mather-era outlook toward connecting visitors with resources. In its early years, the newly formed Park Service encouraged appreciation of remote backcountry areas by allowing park concessioners to erect permanent camps in locations accessible only by trail. The Wilderness Act of 1964 and modern backpacking were still decades in the future when this happened, and the only real alternative at the time was for visitors to charter pack stock. Such camps developed in a number of parks, including Glacier, Grand Canyon, Yosemite, and Sequoia.

Over time the six such camps operating in the High Sierra have become both beloved and reviled. Yosemite sustains five camps accessible only by trail, and Sequoia's Bearpaw facility completes the set. Supplies come in by mule train. None of the camps house more than a few dozen guests at one time (Bearpaw sleeps between twelve and eighteen persons in its six tents), and demand for the space is so strong that reservations often sell out the day the books open for the year. Visitors, usually either well-heeled ex-backpackers or extended family groups, often develop strong affection for the camps and return year after year. They love the experience of walking into the wilderness carrying little more than a toothbrush and change of underwear.

To wilderness purists, the six camps represent perhaps the worst single set of human intrusions into the High Sierra's seemingly pristine wildness. Not only do the camps require permanent structures, but they also need support services such as potable water and wastewater treatment. To the critics, the same luxurious meals, hot showers, and comfortable beds that make the camps so attractive to some flag them as contrary to everything that wilderness stands for. Periodic NPS planning exercises that relate to the future of the camps generate both strong demand for their perpetuation and loud calls for their immediate termination.

I chose sides in this endless dispute years ago after I spent a few weeks in my college years working at Bearpaw. I concluded then that the appreciation the facility generated for the park's backcountry was worth the intrusion. Three decades of subsequent visits have done nothing to change my mind. Even in the modern world of ultralight backpacking, Bearpaw still provides what Stephen Mather envisioned—a way to expose wilderness to a wider audience and build appreciation for it. Ironically, in a time when many wilderness users utilize the High Sierra primarily as a setting for physical endurance challenges, the clientele at Bearpaw continues to focus most of its attention on nature and traditional wilderness values.

The staff at Bearpaw, several among them friends of mine, know that I'm coming, so I surprise no one when I walk up to the kitchen door and lower my pack onto the small porch. Cold beer in hand, I'm soon enjoying once again the camaraderie that the wilderness generates among those who love it. The season is waning and the camp is not full tonight. I've drawn the premier tent platform, which rests on the granite lip of the great canyon immediately to the south of the camp. The screened window of my tent's door frames a classic view of the granite summits of the Great Western Divide. I pull out my last clean socks and underwear and head for the shower house. A homemade wood-burning water heater supplies hot water at Bearpaw, and the two shower stalls occupy a simple wooden structure that resembles nothing much grander than a small garden shed. I've not had a real shower since leaving Bishop, and had no hot water at all since Kern Hot Springs. Now that I'm back in civilization of a sort, I need a bath and I take one.

Half an hour before dinner, I'm sitting on the dining room porch. Life at Bearpaw centers on this small, wood-railed platform. Guests gather here before and after each meal to take in the stupendous view and enjoy each other's company. Most day hikes begin and end here, and some guests spend much of their visits just sitting beneath the canvas awning. The view from the porch takes in the entire southern half of the compass. The foreground drops away quickly into the Yosemite-like depths of River Valley. Just across the canyon, the glacier-scoured peaks of the Great Western Divide rise powerfully to summits twelve thousand feet above the sea. Some of them seem almost close enough to touch. Avalanche-cut furrows add texture to this grand mass of barren rock. On the higher slopes, foxtail pines cling determinedly to windblown ridges where they escape snow slides.

As end-of-the-day shadows lengthen on the peaks, tonight's dinner party assembles. Benches and chairs fill. Beer, wine, and some single-malt scotch appear. Conversations begin. The genius of a place like Bearpaw is that it brings together people who share an interest in nature, provides them with opportunities for adventure, and then sits them down together for family-style meals and talk. Many evenings, the quality of the resulting conversations eclipses even the amazing view. Tonight is no exception. Soon more than a dozen of us are sharing stories.

The dinner bell, a rusty thirty-inch frying pan hanging by kitchen door, rings a welcome call, and we file into the dining room. Canvas provides the roof and walls for this wooden-floored room. Windows, decades old and wood framed, open the room up to the view. We serve ourselves from big platters on a side table and sit down to dine at two long tables. The staff at Bearpaw prides itself on its meals, which are not only hearty but also imaginative. We dine on baked chicken, zucchini, polenta, Spanish rice, and a tomato-and-onion salad. Homemade bread supplements the meal, and dessert completes the menu. Second helpings, and even some thirds, testify to our appetites.

An hour later, the meal consumed, we're back on the porch talking. The good food and wonderful setting make us easy companions. Among this like-minded group, frustration with the nation's culture and political system runs deep. Most feel that our society has lost its conscience when it comes to the natural world. The things we care about, we agree, are less and less important to the larger population and increasingly at risk, and national parks and wilderness head the list. I share some of my thoughts from recent days. We talk about the huge threats to these resources that result from climate change and regional pollution, but I point out that these challenges constitute only half the puzzle. Societal and demographic changes also threaten national parks in fundamental ways.

We live in a society that offers unprecedented opportunities for human experience. Not only do we have leisure time, a concept that did not exist for most only a few generations ago, but we also have an almost infinite number of ways to occupy this time. Even if we

Americans live in a society that works longer hours than most other industrialized nations, we are at the same time profoundly "leisurized." Thousands of activities compete for our attention and money. Many of us define ourselves through our leisure-time choices. We can be professional-football fans, country swing dancers, NASCAR aficionados, or scrapbook fanatics. We can spend our hours playing complex computer games or joining service clubs.

Within our astounding sweep of opportunities, unprecedented in human history, the world of outdoor recreation exists as just another competing lifestyle. Here we find traditional activities like nature appreciation, hunting, and fishing, as well as newer types of entertainment. Seeking to make outdoor recreation more exciting (and profitable), we have invented mountain bikes, snowmobiles, rock climbing, recreational vehicles, downhill skiing, hang gliders, and skateboards we can ride down mountainsides. Like so many other endeavors in our leisurized world, products for most of these activities are actively marketed by commercial interests.

Competing against these largely mechanized outdoor pastimes are less adrenalin-based opportunities like bird watching, hikes on nature trails, and traditional tent camping. These, too, offer leisure lifestyle options, and the participants in these types of sports form the core user group for national parks. What we must perceive is that these lifestyles, which for many of us have associations that merge with moral positions about the importance of nature, are nonetheless just alternative lifestyles among a myriad of such choices.

In the less-developed leisure society of the first half of the twentieth century, the enjoyment of nature and the outdoors rose to near primacy as a popular form of entertainment. Many American families spent their vacations camping; dads took their sons hunting and fishing. Then along came amusement parks, the entertainment *indus-*

try, and destination tourism. Today, as a result of the proliferation of choices, traditional outdoors-based recreation inevitably captures a smaller percentage of the overall leisure market than in times past.

Several parallel trends intensify this effect. Television and the Internet offer forms of indoor mass entertainment that seem particularly attuned to the human psyche, and they have captured enormous amounts of our optional time. Meanwhile, most of the marketing that does exist for outdoor activities comes from businesses that hope to sell expensive equipment like mountain bikes, recreational vehicles, and snowmobiles. These trends come together to create a society in which a smaller and smaller percentage of the population has any real experience in the quieter and less consumptive forms of outdoor recreation. This has significant implications for the future of national parks. Enjoyment of such places requires skills and attitudes that are declining steadily in our population.

Among those who do possess such attitudes and skills, the great majority are found within the white middle class. This should not surprise us. In times past, when outdoor activities filled a larger role in American life, this group formed the nation's demographic core. The use of national parks and wilderness provides particularly strong opportunities for multigenerational outings, and many of us who use parks and wilderness today were first exposed to these places by our parents and grandparents. Such cross-generational training continues today, but the huge influxes of immigrants that have so changed our national demographics in recent decades have brought into our society large numbers of people whose families have no such traditions. As a result, national parks connect to a significantly smaller proportion of the society than a generation ago. Large and growing segments of our population have little or no connection with outdoor recreation in any form.

Richard Louv, in his 2005 book, *Last Child in the Woods,* added an important element to this picture of the changing role of the outdoors in American culture.[11] Louv's thesis, which rings true among those who enjoyed childhoods prior to the 1970s, is that contemporary American children of almost all classes and backgrounds have much less connection to the natural world than their forebearers did. We have separated children from nature, Louv argues, both by providing them with engaging alternatives like television and the Internet and by convincing them that the natural world is dangerous. Also missing from the lives of many children is the simple pleasure of unstructured time spent in the outdoors. All this reflects the culture of fear that has come to dominate America. As parents, we are afraid to allow our children out of our sight, even in nature. The popular media reinforces this message by endlessly hyping the dangers of the world and especially of places we can't control. Out of this endless fear grow separation and, ultimately, profound disinterest. In my last years working as a national park manager, I began to see children watching television in the back of the car as their families toured the national parks. Apparently, neither parents nor children saw any reason why the young folk should even look out the window.

Somehow, despite much anger about how wildlands are being treated, the conversation on the deck at Bearpaw does not descend into bitterness or cynicism. The mood lightens again, and we turn to plans for tomorrow. Only later do I realize that we have spent the entire evening of September 11, 2006, the fifth anniversary of the attacks on New York City and Washington, D.C., without ever mentioning that event. Such is the miracle that is Bearpaw Meadow.

. . .

I arise at first light and savor the trip's last quiet mountain morning. Aside from a low clatter emanating from the kitchen tent, all is still. This fits my mood just fine. Today, after a month in the Sierra's wilderness, I will return to the world that most call civilized. The transition will take me to the Giant Forest, Sequoia National Park's primary visitor feature and the western terminus of the High Sierra Trail. This sequoia grove is not only the place where I first worked in a national park forty years ago but also a troubled landscape where I later spent more than a decade as a park planner wrestling with how to balance preservation and use. Today I want to tie all these things together.

I indulge in a full hot breakfast and prepare to hit the trail. On the way out the door, the ever-friendly Bearpaw staff hands me a sandwich and several thick chocolate brownies. Addresses taken from new friends and good-byes said, I heft my pack and move onto the trail. Truth be told, after last night's socializing I'm looking forward to quiet trail time.

Eleven trail miles separate Bearpaw Meadow from the trailhead at Crescent Meadow, and I've walked this route countless times. In the first mile the High Sierra Trail drops nearly six hundred feet to its crossing of Buck Creek, a major tributary of the Middle Fork of the Kaweah. After that, the trail settles down to pursue a long but reasonably level traverse along the forested slopes of the Kaweah's great Middle Fork Canyon.

I study the forest as I walk. I'm no longer in the high country with its stunted and often snow-twisted stands of pine. Instead, I'm walking through what biologists have long called "Sierra mixed-conifer forest." Between 5,000 and 8,000 feet, the western slope of the Sierra Nevada has a climate that provides conifer trees with both copious moisture and mild winter temperatures. The result, which amazed the first Europeans to experience it, is one of the great softwood forests of the world. Trees grow big here. White and red firs often reach diameters of 3 or 4 feet and heights that exceed 150 feet. Sugar pines grow bigger yet, and then there are the giant sequoias, the world's largest trees, at least by volume. These forest monarchs can exceed 30 feet in diameter, and many tower to 250 feet or more.

Something bad is going on in this forest, however, and not-so-subtle signs are everywhere. Several years ago my eyes began to focus on a change in Sequoia National Park's middle-altitude forests. In laymen's terms, the forests simply didn't look good. Stands that traditionally had been densely green now seemed ratty and battered. When I paid more attention, I saw dead small trees and dying branches on bigger trees: in short—more brown. Pursuing my curiosity, I looked into the issue. I found an alarming answer in research being carried out in the southern Sierra Nevada by the Western Ecological Center of the United States Geological Survey. According to USGS scientists Nate Stephenson and Phil van Mantgem, tree mortality has been increasing dramatically in the southern Sierra's conifer forests over the past twenty years. The two estimate that, for the past several decades, the mortality rate for standing trees has increased roughly 3 percent each year. Most of this mortality has focused on younger trees. Stephenson and van Mantgem hypothesize that this rapid increase in tree death reflects environmental stress resulting from climate change.[12]

To make the situation even more alarming, the two scientists point out that most of this increased mortality has come about during a time of relatively healthy precipitation. What will happen when the next big drought hits the southern Sierra, they ask? A likely outcome, it occurs to me, could be large-scale forest failure, the sort of ecological collapse that occurred early in the twenty-first century in the coniferous mountain forests of Southern California, Arizona, and New Mexico. No wonder the forest looks different. The environmental conditions that created the great conifer forests of Sequoia National Park may no longer exist. Disturbances to the forest that once cleansed it and made it work—processes like insects and lightning-caused fires—may now produce entirely different results.

Life in this forest depends on these trees in so many ways. The woodpeckers are busy today. I see several species. White-headed woodpeckers work the sugar pines, extracting seeds from the cones. I catch glimpses of several red-breasted sapsuckers in the foliage. I flush a northern flicker from the ground where it has been digging for its lunch. A large, dead white fir snag shows the deep scars that come from a pileated woodpecker's efforts to feed on the insects that are helping dismantle this tree skeleton. In a quiet way, this great forest teems with life. I try to imagine it coming apart, disintegrating into something else. Scientifically, such an outcome seems inevitable. Emotionally, I struggle to grasp the idea; this is a national park, after all, a protected place. More than that, for most of my adult life it has been *my* national park, the dream I have spent decades trying to sustain.

By midafternoon my destination is almost in sight. As it approaches the Crescent Meadow trailhead, the High Sierra Trail enters the Giant Forest. John Muir named this sequoia grove in the 1870s, in the process certifying it as one of the world's great forests. The largest trees in the world live here. In 1890, when Congress established Sequoia National Park, the three-square-mile grove received protection from lumbermen. By 1903, the government had built a road to the grove to allow visitors to appreciate the trees. In the following decades the grove became a tourist attraction, and, by the early 1930s, a veritable small city had grown among the Big Trees. Several lodging complexes offered a total of almost three hundred cabins for rent on summer nights. A similar number of government-constructed campsites attracted hundreds more visitors. To support this population, which could reach several thousand persons in midsummer, park managers allowed the construction of restaurants, stores, a gas station, curio shops, a post office, employee housing, maintenance facilities, water and sewer lines, and even an amphitheater where visitors could watch bears feed on garbage collected in the campgrounds. Many of these facilities stood immediately adjacent to massive monarch sequoias, resting upon the trees' roots and at risk from huge falling branches.

Park staff eventually sensed that tourism had become as much of a threat to the forest as the lumbermen of the nineteenth century, but early attempts to reduce or remove tourist development from the grove collided with Stephen Mather's vision of what a national park ought to be. Mather deeply believed that his beloved system of national parks would survive only if the American public loved it, and that such affection could be generated only by visitor use. Under such a paradigm, developments like Giant Forest Village represented a necessary compromise.[13]

During the 1930s, longtime park superintendent John R. White negotiated a partial solution. Commercial development would remain in the grove but would be capped at early-1930s levels. Despite its obvious weaknesses, this compromise endured for decades. By the late 1960s, changing conditions forced a reassessment of the situation. For one thing, the tourist infrastructure of the 1930s had worn out. In the meantime, higher levels of park visitation had overwhelmed 1930s-era roads and parking, and the rustic accommodations of the early days no longer met visitor expectations. At the same time, the growing science of ecology provided new ammunition to those wor-

ried about the health of the forest. For the first time, the long-term
ecological health of the grove became a major issue. In the middle
1970s, the Park Service began talking about removing commercial
development from the grove and relocating the park's visitor services
to less-sensitive sites. In 1980, the agency approved a plan to do just
that. Four years later, the park began receiving funds to carry out
that plan. For the next few years, park staff focused on developing
a new hotel site outside the range of the sequoias. It was during this
period, in 1988, that I became the park's lead planner, responsible for
the future of Giant Forest.

I remember the excitement of the decade that followed. Our team
completed the infrastructure at the new lodge site, negotiated a con-
tract with a concessioner to construct and operate the new facility,
and then turned its attention to the Giant Forest. In the late 1990s
we tore down more than 280 buildings, removed a million square
feet of asphalt, and developed new interpretive facilities, including
a museum that opened in 2001. We imagined we were securing the
foreseeable future of the grove. By removing the excesses of the
Mather-Albright era, we believed we were restoring the national
park dream to its full glory. As a result of our efforts, we hoped, the
Giant Forest could and would be "preserved unimpaired" for future
generations.

Looking back now, I realize how simplistic our vision was. In
restoring the Giant Forest we did indeed solve major problems, but
they were the problems of the twentieth century. At the beginning
of that century, our nation perceived threats to the natural world as
individual and immediate. The giant sequoias would survive if we
could only stop the men with axes. By the later part of the twentieth
century, the national park world had moved on to a broader paradigm, one based on ecosystems and region. Under this model, the

sequoias would survive if we reduced the impacts of visitors and sustained the local processes that affected the ecosystem. Pursuing this model, we removed commercial development from the Giant Forest.

In the twenty-first century, another paradigm is coming into focus. Threats to the sequoias are not just local or regional threats. Park managers must also face profound changes in global patterns of climate as well as numerous other negative factors, including regional and global patterns of pollution and the fragmenting of the natural world into small biological islands. Intensifying all this is the fading societal interest in the natural world. The problems of the past suddenly look small and insignificant. Preserving the sequoias in this new century will require solutions we have barely begun to imagine.

I arrive at Eagle View, a popular destination for day-hikers, and set my pack down. Only one last easy mile separates me from the end of my 240-mile hike. Behind me the granite peaks of the Great Western Divide rise into the sky. A hazy veil of smog softens their profiles. To the west, a thick brown cloud smothers my foothills home and the country beyond. Pulling out my binoculars, I sight my house, six air miles down-canyon and barely visible through the polluted air. I'm ready to end this trip, ready to return to the world of creature comforts and enjoy the company of my wife. I reshoulder my pack and head down the trail toward civilization and all it entails. Around me, the giant sequoias rise into the sky.

FOUR

National Parks
in the Twenty-first Century

Artwork by Matthew J. Rangel, from *a transect—due east*

I set out to walk the familiar trails of the Sierra Nevada in order to seek fresh insights into the increasing divergence I sensed between the mainstream explanations of what national parks and wilderness promise and a new and more somber reality. As I walked, I found even more to worry about. By almost any measure, the world is becoming ever more challenging for our traditional national parks and the resources they promise to preserve forever.

Little that I discovered can be considered completely new. A substantial technical literature focuses on the scientific and philosophical problems that challenge the future of our national parks.[1] Influential as these books have been among park professionals, they have done little to modify the public's investment in the national park covenant—the promise that what we love will not change. Federal managers preparing environmental assessments are required to consider the question of the cumulative impact of all the issues affecting national parks—the synergistic total of all the factors in play. Sadly, the big question of cumulative impact has been largely ignored by the public and even by many who manage the parks. Perhaps the national park dream is simply too powerful. We just don't want to know how much trouble our parks are in.

Problems seldom go away because we refuse to recognize them. In this world of pervasive change, not only are individual national parks in trouble but—and more important—so is the national park idea. Taken together, the issues that threaten national parks in the twenty-first century form an integrated challenge to the national park concept as we know it. Those who are concerned about the fate of our preserved American wildlands must face a full suite of unpalatable truths. Foremost among these is the need to rethink what national parks can be. If national parks are to survive in any significant form, their mission and management goals must be redefined, and that redefinition endorsed and accepted by the American public. The parks will have to undergo a metamorphosis that provides them with both new management goals in tune with our contemporary scientific knowledge and a redefined societal role that attracts new generations of users. Nothing less will succeed.

Historians point out that ideas, and the organizations associated with them, can age and lose their relevance. Today, as the National Park Service approaches the centennial of its establishment in 1916, the agency faces huge potential problems with both its mission and its land management policies. *Senescence* is not too strong a word to apply to the agency and its core mission.

This is not to say there has been no effort to change the agency's paradigms. As mentioned earlier, during the George W. Bush administration the political appointees at the Interior Department, which oversees the NPS, initiated an effort to do just that. Sadly, the effort had little to do with new discoveries in science or even the changing demography of America. Instead, it aimed primarily at increasing economic activity in and around the parks. In one part of this effort, much larger numbers of snowmobiles were authorized to enter Yellowstone National Park. Another effort sought to rewrite portions of the agency's *Management Policies* in a way that would make recreation and development at least coequal with the preservation of park resources—a doctrine that would have turned the National Park Service Organic Act of 1916 on its head.

These efforts did not succeed, mainly because many informed citizens stood up in opposition to defend the national park mission as they knew it. But this successful defense of the parks came at a political cost. While the NPS and its friends were enmeshed in fighting off commercialization, the need to reassess the park system's longer-term goals stayed on the back burner. Despite the efforts of a handful of forward-looking individuals, the service as a whole has been too threatened and too wedded to its traditions to evolve effectively.

Driven by an ideological belief set that rejected science when it did not provide the desired answers, political appointees in the Interior Department during the long years of the George W. Bush administration openly delayed meaningful responses when it came to issues like climate change. The weakness of this approach finally became clear in the summer of 2007, when the U.S. Government Accountability Office issued a report on climate change and federal land management.[2] Responding to a bipartisan request from senators John McCain and John Kerry, the report laid out a strong indictment. After conducting a yearlong study and consulting with the National Academies, the GAO concluded that federal land management agencies, including both the National Park Service and the U.S. Forest Service, had "not made climate change a priority." Neither had the agencies addressed climate change in their strategic plans.

As a part of its response to the GAO during the preparation of the report, the Interior Department resurrected once again the traditional national park management philosophies that had been in place since the 1960s. The department assured the investigators that "natural resources will be managed to preserve fundamental physical and biological processes and maintain all of the components and processes of naturally evolving park ecosystems."[3] In other words, according to the Interior Department, everything was OK. But many on the ground knew what the department would not say out loud: that things were far from OK in the national parks, and that the promises were largely empty rhetoric.

Within the working ranks of the NPS are many who understand this. In the meeting rooms of the agency's regional offices and parks, worried managers, scientists, and partners are trying to determine how to proceed in a world where past assumptions are dissolving. Many realize that issues like climate change present unprecedented challenges to natural resource preservation, park management, and park philosophy.[4] They understand that the old answers no longer work. But all too often when the agency speaks to the public through its interpretive and public affairs programs, the old positions still hold. The same promises still form the core of the agency's *Management Policies;* the dreams of 1916 remain central to the agency's mission and reputation.

The National Park Service can no longer claim to be a young organization. Public discussion about how its centennial should be marked has already begun. Half a century ago, as the agency approached the golden anniversary of its founding, the Park Service envisioned and successfully marketed an initiative known as Mission 66. In those years, NPS managers believed the agency's problems were mostly about not having adequate visitor facilities. Over the course of a decade, Mission 66 financed construction of numerous new visitor centers, campgrounds, bathrooms, maintenance yards, and ranger residences. Nearly all these facilities remain in use today. What Mission 66 did not address was the need for the agency to reinvent itself intellectually in order to catch up with new scientific discoveries.

Fortunately, at the same time, even as the mainstream management of the agency focused on facility improvement, a few farsighted leaders in the Park Service and the Interior Secretary's office commissioned efforts that led to the Leopold Report and the report by the National Academy of Sciences. The contents of these reports, even though resisted initially by many park managers, led the NPS, over time, into a new age of natural resources management. By adopting the management doctrine that preserving natural processes would lead to natural results, and thus unimpaired resources, NPS natural resources management programs attempted to catch up with the biological sciences. This redefinition of *how* to achieve the national park dream on the ground allowed the promise of unimpairment to remain firmly established as the agency's long-term goal.

Half a century later, the situation, the problem, and the opportunity remain much the same. Once again, science has moved on and left national park policy behind. The cutting-edge management philosophies of the 1960s now ring false. "Natural" processes cannot lead reliably to "natural" results in a world where anthropogenic climate change, global pollution, and habitat fragmentation have changed the operating rules, and where society's very definition of *nature* is no longer clear. At the same time, the Park Service, working with the Interior Secretary and NPS friends in Congress, has begun marketing a "centennial challenge." Like Mission 66, this new initiative will focus primarily on improving facilities and sustaining visitor services. Nowhere in its preliminary proposals is there anything significant about reviewing and renewing the agency's intellectual paradigms. But just as in the 1960s, new ideas and policies are badly needed.

. . .

The past teaches us that, when an organization becomes mired in its own traditions, the best way for it to infuse itself with fresh ideas is to listen to outside critics. I have had the good fortune to count one such imaginative critic as both coworker and friend.

After my hike I sought out Dr. Nate Stephenson, a research ecologist with the Biological Resources Division of the United States Geological Survey, to talk further about the future of national parks. Nate has spent three decades studying the ecology of the southern Sierra Nevada, and as early as the mid-1980s he began to consider what a warming climate might do to the ecosystems of the Sierra parks. As he worked on that problem and pondered the results, he also began to seek a new vision of how the biological resources of Sequoia, Kings Canyon, and Yosemite might best be managed in a world of pervasive and inescapable change. Over time, his perspectives have grown into a philosophical vision for the management of national parks in a changing world.

From Stephenson's perspective, the traditional mission of the National Park Service can be likened to "a dinosaur that must evolve or die." By this he means that the time has come for a thorough reconsideration of both the mission of national parks and how that mission is applied to the agency's natural resources. Stephenson's analysis begins from the long-established position that the national park mission is to preserve park resources "unimpaired for the enjoyment of future generations," which is currently defined as restoring and maintaining naturally functioning ecosystems. When this cannot be done, he reminds us, the official policy is to maintain the ecosystems in the "closest approximation" possible of their "natural condition."

As an ecologist, Stephenson finds evidence nearly everywhere that destabilizing change in natural systems is accelerating quickly as a result of human activity. He cites powerful evidence documenting not only well-known large-scale trends like climate change but also less publicized processes like nitrogen deposition, which, as he points out, confirm how completely humans have changed how ecosystems work. He quotes data documenting the reality that, by the last decade of the twentieth century, human beings were generating more biologically active nitrogen, a key plant nutrient, than all natural processes combined. Equally significant to Stephenson are the worldwide effects of nonnative species invasions and habitat fragmentation.

Having demonstrated that maintaining ecosystems free of human effects has become impossible, Stephenson turns his analytical attention to the Park Service's fall-back policy of maintaining impaired systems in the "closest approximation of the natural condition" when they can no longer be sustained unimpaired.[5] Using his ecological knowledge, he points out potential problems with this goal. Humans managing these already damaged systems may find themselves stumbling deep into the realm of unintended consequences. Artificially sustained ecological systems are likely, Stephenson believes, to be inherently unstable and unpredictable. Attempts to "freeze" these systems in a certain state through direct intervention may instead result in the sudden catastrophic loss of key and other desirable ecological elements. Such managed systems may well cross unanticipated thresholds beyond which no amount of direct management will be able to sustain or restore them.

Stephenson offers an experimental vision for the future of ecosystem and landscape management in national parks. Instead of seeking merely to perpetuate already changing ecosystems in as "natural" a state as possible, Stephenson advocates experimenting with a new approach that reflects both his own research and pioneering work done by others. Key to this new strategy are the concepts of resistance and resilience.

Stephenson defines *resistance* as "the ability to resist stress," and *resilience* as "the ability to recover from stress" and thus return to the desired previous condition.[6] By managing in a way that aims for the twin goals of resistance and resilience, Stephenson believes, it may be possible to achieve what he deems must be a primary national park goal of the twenty-first century: perpetuation of as much as possible of the native biodiversity found today in our preserved wildlands.

In these ideas we find the beginnings of a new possible definition of the national park dream, a vision telling us what preservation management can accomplish in this new century. If "unimpaired" is now beyond us, at least in the sense that it meant originally, we can still manage to save much of the amazing diversity of life that exists in our parks. But to do so we will have to think and act in a fundamentally different manner. We must not only redefine the purpose of national parks but also reconsider our concepts of nature and wildness.

As the term is used by natural resource managers in the national parks, *nature* has acquired a number of related but distinct meanings. Core to most understandings of "nature" and "natural" are the twin concepts of a biological world that is both unaffected and unmanaged by humans. A biological world such as this results, according to traditional thinking, in biological systems that are "stable, self-regulating, and equilibrial." Implied also is a "high degree of historical fidelity."[7]

Knowing what we now know about not only the current state of the earth's biosystems but also how profoundly humans affected ecosystems even in times past, this broad definition of nature no longer provides a useful concept. A century ago we believed that much that occurred on the planet went on outside of human control. Now, we know better. With the exception, perhaps, of the grand tectonic processes that shape the earth's surface, almost nothing is now beyond our potential influence. Contemporary science tells us that we humans have the capacity to extirpate many of our fellow life-forms, melt the polar icecaps, shift huge oceanic currents, and even modify the genes that determine the nature of life. More daunting yet is that we appear incapable of preventing ourselves from doing many of these things. In such a humanized world, what validity can the traditional definition of "natural" retain? Is there a world left that is both unmanaged and unaffected by humans? The answer, of course, is no.

In the world we humans have created, we have reached the point where the two concepts of management and effect must be separated. If there remains little that is unaffected by humans, can there still be significant resources that remain unmanaged and self-governing?

Poet and essayist Gary Snyder has wrestled with this question. In his 1990 book *The Practice of the Wild,* he explored the nuances that separate the concepts of "natural" and "wild."[8] Drawing on numerous sources, including his own deep involvement in Asian philosophy, Snyder defined significant differences between the two ideas. Although *nature* is often used to imply the outdoors, or the "world apart from human will," Snyder pointed out, the best definitions of "nature" see it as the complete physical world that we inhabit. By this definition, our cities and agricultural lands are as natural as our national parks or wilderness areas. In contrast to *nature,* Snyder set forth the idea of *the wild.* Wrestling with this concept that he found as elusive as "a gray fox trotting off through the forest," he built a definition that places *the wild* outside human management. To Snyder, *the wild* is a state in which animals live their lives as free agents and where plants propagate and organize themselves independently. It is a world unmanaged by humans. As we think about the world of national parks and preserved lands, perhaps the time has come to step away from a broad concept of nature, with all its baggage, and instead focus more closely on the idea of *wild* and the concept of biological systems marching forward unregulated by human activity.

Significantly, part of the confusion facing the Park Service in the twenty-first century derives from its defined policies that speak about much that ought to be natural, but about nothing that is specifically wild. The latter concept, in fact, plays no defined role in the service's philosophical vocabulary. The agency's management policies and organizational structure place major emphasis on *natural* resources but say little about wildness as a distinct attribute of landscapes or ecosystems. As used by the NPS, *natural* incorporates Snyder's concept of *the wild,* as well as the associated traditional concepts of ecosystems that not only remain unaffected by humans but also are stable and self-regulating and retain historical integrity. Mixed within this swirl of ideas is the agency's working definition of *impairment.*

Unfortunately, we can no longer prevent the impairment of our traditional national parks, at least in the sense that the National Park Service and the act of 1916 promise. As my hike taught me, even geographically remote landscapes are no longer beyond the scope of human dominance. But a new approach is worth considering, an approach that marries the goals of preserving native biodiversity and of embracing wildness. Such a mix will not come easily. Finding a working balance between managing to preserve biodiversity and perpetuating elements of true wildness will require unprecedented experimentation. Stephenson sees resistance and resilience as useful tools in this experiment. He is providing, as he puts it, not a set of goals but only a means to an end. That end, as he sees it, is the circumstance of "buying time and preventing sudden catastrophic loss while ecosystems rearrange themselves with or without human help." Rather than moving forward under the 1916 assumption that everything can and must be saved, managers would recognize instead that everything is at risk and much is likely to be lost. Management would continue to seek to minimize intrusive threats such as chemical pollution, invasive species, and disrupted fire regimes, but this work would be conducted within a context that accepts the inevitability of change.

Such an approach would move forward not by assuming the ecological world is stable but rather by anticipating the unexpected. Monitoring, in this model, would inform a feedback loop intended to help managers preserve as much native biodiversity as possible. Wildland fires, for example, would be closely monitored to determine whether they lead to the perpetuation of biodiversity or tend toward the reduction of ecosystems into landscapes dominated by a handful of disturbance-dependent ("weedy") species. Proactive management elements that today would be clearly rejected, such as facilitating the migration of native species to new locales where they might survive in a changing climate regime, would become acceptable. The long-held dream of restoring damaged ecosystems to some preindustrial condition would be abandoned as usually impossible.

Such an approach is sharply at odds with traditional National Park Service policy. In the most recent edition of the agency's *Management Policies*, a key section still requires park managers to preserve *all* components and processes, including "the natural abundance, diversity, and genetic and ecological integrity of the plant and animals species native to those ecosystems." The same paragraph forbids management to enhance individual species, with the exception of listed threatened and endangered species.[9] Laudable as they may be, such policies are likely doomed to fail in a world where human-caused ecosystem change has become both pervasive and inescapable.

Implied here is a degree of hands-on management of natural resources that rejects the nineteenth-century assumptions of the national park movement's founders. They assumed that we could sustain the biological landscapes we valued simply by preventing immediate damage and then leaving them alone. A new vision of national parks must come to grips with the idea that in many cases we are most likely to save those elements that we actively manage. This implies not only a fundamental reversal of our relationship to the ecological world but also an endless cascade of painful and difficult choices.

Such an approach will also run the risk of placing natural resource management programs in direct conflict with *wildness* as a state of being. Accepting *wildness* as a key goal implies accepting unmanaged change and its results. But what if the resulting changes lead away from biodiversity? What if *wildness* in a world sorely wounded by global-scale human activity leads to ecological simplification and loss? On the ground, the tension between these two goals will be difficult to resolve. Finding a workable balance will require continuous resource monitoring, thoughtful analysis, and much on-the-ground experimentation.

Embedded within this complex puzzle is a possibility of hope few nonscientists recognize. The very science that discloses the severity of the damage we are inflicting on the earth's biological systems also provides new and powerful tools for analyzing experimental management techniques. Compared to managers of decades past, we possess an unprecedented ability to understand the impacts of our actions. Tools like remote sensing and global positioning give us the power to collect data that was impossible to gather during the twentieth century. At the same time, computers give us the ability to process and organize this data in new and complex ways. Far better than in years past, it is now possible to evaluate our impacts. This will have value, however, only if we accept that scientific data must trump ideology as a basis for decision making.

In the end, the menu of conceptual options for managing the wildlands of our traditional national parks is surprisingly short. The experimental strategy that Stephenson proposes might best be summarized as "managing for change." The underlying logic assumes that the best path will be to study the processes of ecosystem and landscape change and then actively seek ways to preserve the things we value in this changing world. But there are many professionals in the Park Service who recoil from Stephenson's management prescriptions. They point out, citing much history, that attempts to manipulate ecosystems have seldom led to the desired results. How do we know, they ask, that we won't just make a bad situation worse? Many in this school of thought urge the Park Service to stick to its path of minimal intervention, to a path that emphasizes *wildness*. Much will change, they admit, and things will be lost, but letting ecosystems find their own solutions will work best in the long run.

This school defines a clear alternative path centered on accepting *the wild* as the primary guiding premise. In this approach, managers would step back from active management and allow natural systems to evolve toward new states. By definition, whatever resulted from wildness would be a success.

Sequoia National Park's Giant Forest offers a useful setting for considering how these two approaches might play out. The famous giant sequoia grove where I ended my hike features old-growth sequoias in a complex mixed-conifer forest setting. Preserving this forest ecosystem intact in the form we found it in the nineteenth century may already be impossible. Tree mortality within the existing old-growth stands has been increasing for decades and has now at least doubled. Applying our concept models demonstrates the complexity of the challenge before us. As the climate warms, the sequoia species (and many other species in the grove) might benefit from help

that would facilitate their moving not only upslope in the immediate vicinity but also northward in the Sierra Nevada to entirely
new locations outside the parks. Pursuing a strategy of "managing
for change," park staff would assist this shift. In contrast, managers
pursuing a "wild" strategy would take no active role but would accept
the changes that did occur and define them as appropriate. Judging
from paleoclimatic research, this path might lead to a substantial
reduction in giant sequoia presence in the parks and conceivably
even to the species' eventual extinction.

Both of these approaches would accept the biological imperative
of change, and, from a scientific point of view, either could be justified in a redefined national park setting. But there is something
missing from this equation. As a public relations strategy for national
parks, each approach is profoundly problematic. Either could further
weaken public interest in the parks. Missing here is any appreciation
of the role of the NPS covenant in perpetuating public support for
national parks. Visitors come to Sequoia National Park to see the
Big Trees. Will they still come if the Giant Forest loses its sequoias?
And if they don't come, then what will happen to the park's public
support? An obvious political response would be a third approach,
a localized "ecosystem museum" strategy designed to perpetuate
samples of key resources. Under this strategy, park managers would
attempt to identify and artificially sustain key biological elements in
national parks.

Again, the Giant Forest provides a useful setting for imagining
how this might work. If managed as an ecosystem museum, the Giant
Forest would be actively manipulated to sustain the continued presence of key stands of old-growth giant sequoias. This might involve
supplemental irrigation, removal of invasive species, planting of failing species, and any number of other possible actions. In some ways,

the grove would become an intensively managed botanical garden. Would this work? Scientists point out that it is probably impossible to artificially preserve complete, functioning ecosystems once the environmental conditions that created them have changed. But can key elements of those systems be artificially sustained? The answer, which comes as much from horticulture as from ecology, is *maybe*.

As biologically flawed as the "ecosystem museum" approach may appear, it represents a logical outcome of current NPS policy when applied to the problems of the twenty-first century. As defined by the agency's *Management Policies,* the prescribed NPS response to biological deterioration or collapse is restoration, which often looks a lot like artificial life support for ecosystems. Hawaii Volcanoes National Park provides an interesting example. By the middle years of the twentieth century, it had become apparent that the ecosystems that defined the park's tropical rain forests were unraveling in a catastrophic fashion. The natural systems of Hawaii had evolved many endemic life-forms that prospered in the absence of competition. Once Hawaii lost its geographical isolation, invasive plants and animals moved into these forests and established themselves at the expense of native organisms. The response of the NPS was to initiate an expensive program of ecosystem management that involved both continuous weeding of invasive plants and aggressive suppression of nonnative fauna. This program, which can be seen as an early example of "ecosystem museum" management, has gone on for decades and has succeeded to a significant degree, but at a high and perhaps ultimately unsustainable financial cost. Mitigating the effects of climate change, even on a very small geographical scale, will likely prove harder and even more expensive.

Nonetheless, it is easy to imagine Hawaii Volcanoes National Park's "ecosystem museum" as a model for many other critical national park features. In order to sustain public interest and support, the national parks may have no choice but to manage selected scenic resources in a manner that provides continuity and familiarity to the visiting public. Sometimes, as in the case of the Giant Forest of Sequoia National Park, this will take the form of sustaining key biological resources even if they can no longer survive without human intervention. Other NPS units with famous biologically based identities come to mind here, places like Redwood, Joshua Tree, and Saguaro National Parks.

In other cases, the challenge will be not so much to establish an "ecosystem museum" as to preserve the general appearance of key scenic resources. Yosemite Valley, the High Sierra, Jackson Hole, the lake shores at Glacier, the Yellowstone Plateau, the Grand Canyon: even as these environments change biologically, the NPS may need to manage them in a way that keeps them *feeling* familiar, a management need that would blend together something of wildness, management for change, and ecosystem museums into an entirely new mix. All this will require the politically dangerous but unavoidable necessity of redefining the agency's long-standing covenant with the American public.

Since 1916, national park managers have talked about the "dual mission" of the National Park Service, a mission that requires both preservation of resources and facilitation of the appropriate enjoyment of those same resources. Now, even as the service continues to wrestle with this supposed dichotomy, it may also be faced with a new dualism. This challenge will require the agency to develop the wisdom and the capacity to manage its resources for the long term in new and controversial ways while, at the same time, somehow sustaining selected biological and landscape features that attract public support.

On the ground, is the Park Service capable of preserving giant sequoias as a viable wild species while at the same time sustaining them artificially in situ in a manner that satisfies the needs of tourism? A profound disconnect haunts this question. Attempting to preserve selected fragments of ecosystems may not work as a biological strategy. Doing anything less, however, may fail as a political strategy. And all these proposals assume that funds for management will be forthcoming from Congress, an assumption that becomes ever more tenuous each fiscal year.

Such questions imply that the future management of the landscapes and ecosystems of our national parks will be both more complex and more nuanced than anything seen to date. Perhaps no single approach will meet all of society's needs. Conflicting demands may require that national parks be divided into management zones that allow the Park Service to pursue all three approaches at once but in different areas or even sometimes to blend them together. Supporting this imperfect but probably inescapable compromise is the likelihood that a policy of nonintervention *(the wild)* will inevitably be tested on a massive scale. The reason is simple: Even if the Park Service were to commit fully to a strategy of management for change, it would be hard pressed financially to carry out such a program on more than a small percentage of the acreage contained within its parks. In reality, huge tracts will remain beyond the ability of the agency to manage. These landscapes will go where climate change and other environmental stresses take them. As a default strategy, *the wild* will almost certainly dominate the future of the parks.

What biological role can traditional national parks fulfill in the twenty-first century? A realistic answer to this question requires that we seize what is possible and jettison much that is not. If the parks cannot be untouched islands that preserve the landscapes and ecosystems Europeans found in North America several centuries ago, they can still serve important biological purposes. They can be places where *wildness* survives, where biological diversity is protected and cherished, and where key ecosystem elements are sometimes preserved as living museum pieces. Weaving these contradictory threads together will be difficult, but all these tools will be required to piece together a new national park vision.

. . .

Losing the core tenets of its long-established and highly popular mission will challenge the Park Service every bit as much as finding a new and successful way to manage quickly changing ecosystems. Reduced to the essentials, the question becomes simple: if ecosystems cannot be kept "unimpaired," then what? Answering this question requires, as Stephen Mather knew long ago, that we move even farther into the human side of the puzzle.

Educating the public to accept change is perhaps one of the greatest challenges a government agency can face. For the National Park Service, the challenge is even greater since the agency has so long emphasized to the public that its mission has been to prevent change. This is a position the NPS must abandon. In this changing world, the NPS must begin talking about change as an inescapable part of the park world. Painful as it will be, the Mather-era promise of "unimpaired for future generations" must be replaced with a more realistic vision.

Intensifying the challenge the Park Service faces as it attempts to engage the public in a new mission for national parks is the inescapable fact that the social role of the parks in American society also has been changing.[10] In the Sierra Nevada, annual visitation peaked at Yosemite National Park in 1996 and, for the past decade, has been running 10–15 percent below that level.[11] During the same period many other national parks have suffered similar losses.

Current trends suggest that the recreational role of national parks is likely to continue to shrink. In California, the parks that have been the focus of this book are more difficult to access than several decades ago because of population growth and traffic congestion. At the same time, entire new competing recreational worlds have blossomed. The virtual reality of the digital world offers much that attracts. One can be transported to another realm without having to travel or even sweat. The rewards of engagement are immediate; why go instead to a faraway place that requires a lot of time and special skills to enjoy? Demographic change is critical as well, with growing segments of society having no tradition of national park use or even interest in nature. In many ways, national park experiences are not competing well in the leisure-time market.

Attempting to use these trends as a wedge, interest groups that have long felt excluded from national parks are attempting to manipulate these issues to their advantage. Their voiced goal is to increase recreational use, especially highly profitable forms of mechanized recreational use. More access for those who want to use machines like snowmobiles or trail bikes, the argument goes, will increase park use. Such arguments, unfortunately, make no useful response to key issues like intense competition within the leisure-time market and changing demographics. They ignore statistics that demonstrate that many other outdoors-based activities, including hunting and fishing, are also losing adherents. Making national parks more like other types of public lands seems unlikely to result in the creation of more outdoor recreationists. At best, such a shift might divert some current use away from national forests and toward national parks, but at the cost of losing forever what is special about the parks—the fact that they offer visitor experiences that cannot be found elsewhere.

As a recreational world requiring an investment of time and sweat and the development of special skills, national parks inevitably will continue their evolution toward becoming just another specialized form of outdoor recreation. This reflects not so much a loss of relevance on the part of parks as a maturing of our society's recreational options. At the same time, the parks will continue to offer something unique: wildness and experiences based on genuine, unpredictable reality. That these experiences offer opportunities for beauty and solitude makes them more valuable yet, as does the fact that these same lands can also serve the critical biological role of sustaining biodiversity. No other leisure lifestyle alternative does anything comparable for the benefit of our descendents, and it is upon these values that the future of the national parks rests.

The national parks and those who care about them must face the necessity of marketing the values and unique experiences associated with national parks in the competitive leisure-time world of the twenty-first century. Stephen Mather knew this a century ago, and now, as Mather's agency approaches its centennial in 2016, the challenge remains. National parks will survive as significant institutions only if they are appreciated and supported by an informed citizenry who understands their purpose and supports their management. Selling larger segments of society on the value of places where the long-advertised mission is no longer possible, where resources seem to be unraveling, where quality experiences require preacquired skills and knowledge to enjoy, and where significant blocks of time are required to recreate, will be anything but easy. Add the complication that this marketing must be successful with many families that have little or no tradition of national park use or interest in nature, and the challenge becomes daunting. But there is no choice. In our society, ideas that do not compete effectively usually fade and die.

In the autumn of 2009, the preeminent documentary filmmaker Ken Burns addressed this very question. In a twelve-hour-long PBS special, *The National Parks: America's Best Idea,* Burns, together with Dayton Duncan, his production partner and the series' writer, created a value-defined view of the national parks that sought in subtle ways to redefine the significance of the parks and their story. Instead of focusing primarily on Mather's historic but now troubled covenant, Burns and Duncan sought to position the national parks as a key expression of American democracy. In carefully measured segments, they expounded their theme that the publicly owned parks, set aside for the benefit of all, are indeed our republic's best expression of its true nature. Carefully omitted was any suggestion that the parks were based on an unattainable goal.

Embedded in the National Park Service Organic Act of 1916, in the same section as the famous language about conserving the parks "unimpaired for the enjoyment of future generations," is another, much-less quoted clause that instructs the Park Service to "promote" national parks. As perceptive critics like Denny Galvin and Robin Winks have noted, this legal instruction has received very little attention over the years. In the context of 1916, "promoting" national parks reflected Stephen Mather's worldview that parks needed to be widely used if they were to be loved and supported. In the twenty-first century a different meaning offers itself. Pondering this question, Denny Galvin recently concluded: "There remains a need to promote the parks, not to bring people to them, but to promulgate the values they have come to represent."[12]

The values Galvin emphasizes here rise far above management

policies. In a culture that accepts accelerating human consumption of the earth as a necessity, and where the natural world means less and less to each succeeding generation, national parks remain the best place to share the knowledge that will allow us to sustain life on this earth. Somewhere on this ever-more-humanized planet, we still need landscapes and ecosystems that remind us of our biological and cultural origins. In such places we can still "ground" ourselves in the world that created our species. In this new century, where nothing natural or wild seems beyond the threatening reach of humankind, the cultural values associated with national parks may ultimately be their most important feature. If "unimpaired for future generations" must be abandoned, a new vision and a new set of values must be offered. Finding words to match the strength of those written nearly a century ago will not be easy, but the key concepts are now clear. A redefinition more in line with our times might read as follows:

> The purpose of said parks shall be to preserve wildness, and as much as possible of the rich biological and cultural heritage of this planet, in a manner that will allow for the sustained and respectful enjoyment of these resources by present and future generations.

I set out hiking from Tuolumne Meadows to renew my understanding of the management goals of our traditional national parks. I had become confused. The long-established mission of these special places no longer seemed possible. The management philosophies I had been taught in my years as a park ranger no longer seemed workable. As a historian, I sensed change in the air: change in places that were intended never to change.

I came out of the High Sierra, some 240 miles and thirty days later, richer in many ways. I found in the high country, as I always have over the decades, great beauty and moments of inner peace. I also found profound change: in biology, in technology, in hiking styles, in management, in society, and in myself. Just as I learned that an older hiker must adapt to the inescapable realities of an aging body, I also learned that national parks and wilderness will have to adapt to the realities of a fundamentally different world. Survival, Darwin discerned a century and a half ago, is ultimately about the ability to adapt. The lesson remains apt.

Is such change truly possible? Can national parks evolve success-fully to survive as significant institutions in a world so profoundly different? The answer to these questions lies with those of us who care about these special places. History gives us reason for hope.

I ended my journey in the Giant Forest of Sequoia National Park, the home of the largest of all the magnificent trees that grow on this planet. In the five generations since Californians of European descent first encountered these amazing organisms, they have moti-vated our society repeatedly.

Barely a decade after their initial discovery in 1852, sequoia trees helped inspire the Yosemite grant, the first federal action to set aside lands in a form resembling a modern national park. Less than thirty years later, in 1890, this same species inspired Californians to cam-paign successfully for the creation of three national parks, an effort that began our nation's shift from having a single national park to having a national park system. Today, that system has nearly four hundred units.

The sequoias played so important a role in the early days of the national parks that, in the years following 1916, the new agency chose the sequoia cone as its emblem. Even today, in the service's tenth decade, every national park ranger still has sequoia cones embossed on the leather of his or her uniform belt and hatband.

In the middle years of the twentieth century, the ecological needs of sequoias redefined the park idea and forced land managers to come to grips with the necessity of revolutionizing our relationship with ecological processes like wildland fire. Out of this came not only the modern program of managed wildland fire for environmental purposes but also much of the rest of contemporary natural resources management philosophy. In the late years of the twentieth century, the Big Trees inspired the Park Service to remove a century's accumulation of commercial development from the Giant Forest, one of the boldest acts of restoration yet undertaken in a national park.

Now, the time has come for the sequoias to inspire us once again. Perhaps these grand trees, which have challenged us repeatedly and brought out the best in our culture, will again work their magic. This time they challenge us to reinvent our national parks to fit a profoundly changing world and to convince our democracy to support that new direction. The survival of our parks as significant public institutions will depend on our ability to do exactly that.

NOTES

INTRODUCTION

1. "The service thus established shall promote and regulate the use of the Federal areas known as national parks, monuments, and reservations hereinafter specified by such means and measures as conform to the fundamental purpose of the said parks, monuments, and reservations, *which purpose is to conserve the scenery and the natural and historic objects and the wildlife therein and to provide for the enjoyment of the same in such manner and by such means as will leave them unimpaired for the enjoyment of future generations.*" U.S.C., title 16, sec. 1, "An Act to Create a National Park Service," italics added.

2. Ibid.

ONE. SOUTH FROM YOSEMITE

1. An Act to Set Apart Certain Tracts of Land in the State of California as Forest Reservations (October 1, 1890), sec. 2. Not until 1906 would the state and federal reservations be merged to create the modern Yosemite National Park.

2. Wilderness Act of 1964 (Public Law 88–577), sec. 2(c).

3. Ibid.

4. Short-hair sedge, *Carex filifolia,* dominates huge acreages within the Sierra's high country, yet few hikers seem to notice it.

5. The contemporary literature on this subject not only contradicts the Virgin Continent perspective but also proposes in its place something far more complex: landscapes that were not wild at all but rather were intensively managed to produce desired results. The pre-European-contact residents of California, this research suggests, used processes such as fire, vegetative pruning, and stream damming to modify landscapes and make them more productive. In the High Sierra, where biological productivity is not as high as at lower altitudes, these effects were somewhat reduced but still significant. See Anderson, *Tending the Wild.*

6. For a good summary of this scholarship, see Mann, *1491.* Diamond's *Guns, Germs, and Steel* places the story in a broader historical context.

7. In what would be his last major journey, John Muir traveled to South America and Africa in 1911–1912. As a part of this trip, he took the train north from Cape Town in South Africa to Rhodesia, Mozambique, and Kenya. In recent years, his notes and journals from the trip have been published. In them Muir documents what he saw as he looked out the windows of his railcars. He notes mostly trees and geology. In his journal he says almost nothing about the native peoples or the British and Portuguese colonial administrations. Apparently Muir saw Africa through the same Virgin Continent lens that he applied to North America. See Branch, *John Muir's Last Journey.*

8. In the first half of the twentieth century, as the national park system came into being, and despite the ravages of microbes and racist invaders, remnant populations of native peoples remained in a number of western national parks, including Yosemite, Grand Canyon, and Death Valley. The National Park Service, perceiving these people as a threat to natural landscapes, worked hard to force them out of the parks, an effort that largely succeeded. For a particularly good exploration of the modern history of native peoples in Yosemite, see Spence, *Dispossessing the Wilderness.* Also of interest is Keller and Turek, *American Indians and National Parks.*

9. Jensen, "More Large Forest Fires Linked to Climate Change."

TWO. KINGS CANYON NATIONAL PARK

1. See Solomons, "Beginnings of the John Muir Trail"; and Sargent, *Solomons of the Sierra*.

2. The NPS did not begin to employ even a few wildlife biologists until the late 1920s, and funding for that initial effort came from outside the agency. See Sellars, *Preserving Nature in the National Parks*.

3. See McClelland, *Building the National Parks*.

4. Leopold, "Wildlife Management in the National Parks"; and National Academy of Sciences, National Research Council, *Report by the Advisory Committee to the National Park Service on Research*.

5. In *Windshield Wilderness*, a useful study focusing on the Pacific Northwest, David Louter explores how the national park idea evolved in that region and elsewhere. Louter makes it clear that the national park idea has evolved significantly over time.

6. United States Department of the Interior, National Park Service, *Management Policies 2006*, sec. 4.4.1.

7. Over the years since his death, Muir has inspired numerous biographies. The most recent comes from the eminent environmental historian Donald Worster: *Passion for Nature*.

8. A broad view of the current status of the Sierra's frog life can be found in Gee, Stansfield, and Clayburgh, *State of Sierra Frogs*.

9. Cohen, *History of the Sierra Club*, 9; and Le Conte, "Among the Sources of the South Fork of the King's River—Part I," and "Part II."

10. The need for a new biography of Mather, one that addresses his founding role in terms of how the national park system and National Park Service have turned out, is obvious. Shankland's laudatory 1951 biography, *Steve Mather of the National Parks*, remains the primary source. Horace Albright's 1985 remembrance, *Birth of the National Park Service*, fills in some of the gaps. More are addressed in Albright's succeeding work on the subject, coauthored by Marian Albright Schenck, *Creating the National Park Service*.

11. United States Department of the Interior, National Park Service, *Management Policies 2006*, 2.

12. Blehm, *Last Season*.

13. United States Forest Service, *Use of the National Forests.*

14. See chapter 5 of Dilsaver and Tweed, *Challenge of the Big Trees.*

15. Randall, *Report to the Federal Power Commission on the Storage Resources of the South and Middle Forks of the Kings River, California.*

16. Some in the club supported the Forest Service initially, hoping that the agency would find the area an appropriate place to experiment with the new concept of setting aside forestlands as wilderness.

17. On May 8, 2008, nearly two years after I completed my hike, United States magistrate judge Elizabeth Laporte issued a final injunction effectively resolving these issues. In her decision, Laporte concluded that the Forest Service, in its pack-stock management program, had violated both the Wilderness Act and the National Environmental Policy Act. Her injunction voided a number of Forest Service procedures and established new limits and controls on where and when pack stock could be used, and on how many animals could enter the wilderness over the course of the summer. These new court-established limits were not as stringent as those requested by the High Sierra Hikers Association or as generous as those recommended by the Forest Service and the Backcountry Horsemen.

18. Now more than a century old, Stewart Edward White's *Camp and Trail* still provides useful insight into the traditional world of packing in the Sierra Nevada and elsewhere.

19. See Stegner's introduction to *Wildlands in Our Civilization,* by David Brower, 33–43.

20. Muir's Sierra Nevada exploits are well documented. Marshall focused his sometimes almost maniacal passion for wilderness motion on landscapes well removed from the Sierra Nevada, including particularly the Adirondacks, the northern Rockies, and Alaska. See Glover, *Wilderness Original.*

21. Later, we will find out that a ranger searching from a helicopter discovered the body of the missing solo hiker on the steep northern cliffs of Mount Brewer, the very mountain we saw on the horizon from Glen Pass.

22. Wilderness Act of 1964 (Public Law 88–577), sec. 2(c).

23. Brower, *Wilderness,* 24.

THREE. SEQUOIA NATIONAL PARK

1. Louter, David. *Windshield Wilderness.*

2. The competition continues for unsupported speed travel over the John Muir Trail. As of July 2009, the record time belonged to Michael Popov, who made the trip in 2007 in four days, five hours, and twenty-five minutes. See www.southernmostrunners.com/JMT/AaronsJMTStory-07.htm.

3. An eyewitness account of these tragic events exists in Griffin, "Trail Building in the High Sierras."

4. For an interesting insight into the world of military flight training over the wilderness, see United States Department of Defense, *R-2508 Complex User's Handbook.*

5. Diaz and Eischeid, "Disappearing 'Alpine Tundra' Köppen Climatic Type in the Western United States."

6. United States Department of the Interior, National Park Service, *Management Policies 2006,* 1.4.4 through 1.4.7.1.

7. Leopold, *Round River,* 165.

8. Recent decades have added Redwood, Joshua Tree, and Saguaro National Parks to the list.

9. In 2007, according to the California Department of Pesticide Regulation, farmers applied 15,319,425 pounds of restricted-use chemicals to lands in Tulare County, and another 36,082,330 pounds in neighboring Fresno County.

10. In this context, the NPS defines *impairment* as an impact to a park resource "that would harm the integrity of park resources or values." For more details on this critical definition, see section 1.4.5 of *Management Policies 2006.*

11. Louv, *Last Child in the Woods.*

12. Van Mantgem and Stephenson, "Apparent Climatically Induced Increase of Tree Mortality Rates in a Temperate Forest."

13. The long history of wrestling with the question of how to manage the Giant Forest is detailed in Dilsaver and Tweed, *Challenge of the Big Trees.* See especially chaps. 6 and 8.

FOUR. NATIONAL PARKS
IN THE TWENTY-FIRST CENTURY

1. See, for example, Cronon, *Uncommon Ground;* Botkin, *Discordant Harmonies* and *No Man's Garden;* and Worster, *Wealth of Nature.*

2. United States Government Accountability Office, *Climate Change: Agencies Should Develop Guidance for Addressing the Effect on Federal Lands and Water Resources.*

3. Ibid.

4. A perceptive summary of contemporary thought on this question can be found in Cole et al., "Naturalness and Beyond," 36–56.

5. United States Department of the Interior, National Park Service, *Management Policies 2006,* sec. 4.1.

6. For more on the origins of these concepts, see Hansen, Biringer, and Hoffman, *Buying Time.*

7. Cole et al., "Naturalness and Beyond," 38.

8. Snyder, *Practice of the Wild,* 8–18.

9. United States Department of the Interior, National Park Service, *Management Policies 2006,* 4.1.

10. Pergams and Zaradic provide useful context for this issue in their "Evidence for a Fundamental and Pervasive Shift away from Nature-Based Recreation."

11. A major flood in Yosemite Valley in January 1997 damaged and closed a number of visitor facilities and has often been blamed for Yosemite's drop in visitation. It is apparent, however, that declines in visitor use at Yosemite parallel similar changes in many other national park units.

12. Winks, "Robin Winks on the Evolution and Meaning of the Organic Act"; and Galvin, "Organic Act," 23.

REFERENCES

Albright, Horace M. *The Birth of the National Park Service: The Founding Years, 1913–33*. Salt Lake City: Howe Brothers, 1985.

Albright, Horace M., and Marian Albright Schenck. *Creating the National Park Service: The Missing Years*. Norman: University of Oklahoma Press, 1999.

Anderson, Kat. *Tending the Wild: Native American Knowledge and the Management of California's Natural Resources*. Berkeley: University of California Press, 2005.

Beesley, David. *Crow's Range: An Environmental History of the Sierra Nevada*. Reno: University of Nevada Press, 2004.

Blehm, Eric. *The Last Season*. New York: HarperCollins, 2006.

Botkin, Daniel B. *Discordant Harmonies: A New Ecology for the Twenty-first Century*. Oxford: Oxford University Press, 1992.

———. *No Man's Garden: Thoreau and a New Vision of Civilization and Nature*. Washington, DC: Island Press, 2000.

Branch, Michael P., ed. *John Muir's Last Journey: South to the Amazon and East to Africa*. Washington, DC: Island Press, 2001.

Brower, David, ed. *Wilderness: America's Living Heritage*. San Francisco: Sierra Club, 1961.

———. *Wildlands in Our Civilization*. San Francisco: Sierra Club, 1964.

Browning, Peter. *Place Names of the Sierra Nevada: From Abbot to Zumwalt.* Berkeley, CA: Wilderness Press, 1986.

Cohen, Michael. *The History of the Sierra Club: 1892–1970.* San Francisco: Sierra Club, 1988.

Cole, David N., et al. "Naturalness and Beyond: Protected Area Stewardship in an Era of Global Environmental Change." *George Wright Forum* 25 (2008): 36–56.

Cronon, William, ed. *Uncommon Ground: Rethinking the Human Place in Nature.* New York: W.W. Norton, 1995.

Diamond, Jared. *Guns, Germs, and Steel: The Fates of Human Societies.* New York: W.W. Norton, 1997.

Diaz, Henry F., and Jon K. Eischeid. "Disappearing 'Alpine Tundra' Köppen Climatic Type in the Western United States." *Geophysical Research Letter* 34 (2007): L18707.

Dilsaver, Lary, and William C. Tweed. *Challenge of the Big Trees: A Resource History of Sequoia and Kings Canyon National Parks.* Three Rivers, CA: Sequoia Natural History Association, 1990.

Farquhar, Francis. "Early History of the Kings River Sierra." *Sierra Club Bulletin* 26 (1941): 28–41.

———. *History of the Sierra Nevada.* Berkeley: University of California Press, 1965.

———. "Stephen T. Mather." *Sierra Club Bulletin* 15 (1931): 55–59.

Galvin, Denny. "The Organic Act—a User's Guide: Further Thoughts on Winks' 'A Contradictory Mandate?'" *George Wright Forum* 24 (2007): 22–25.

Gee, Marion, Sara Stansfield, and Joan Clayburgh. *State of Sierra Frogs: A Report on the Status of Frogs and Toads in the Sierra Nevada and California Cascade Mountains.* South Lake Tahoe, CA: Sierra Nevada Alliance, 2008.

Glover, James M. *A Wilderness Original: The Life of Bob Marshall.* Seattle: The Mountaineers, 1986.

Griffin, Donald. "Trail Building in the High Sierras." Manuscript in the author's collection, 1990.

Hansen, L.J., J.L. Biringer, and J.R. Hoffman. *Buying Time: A User's Manual for Building Resistance and Resilience to Climate Change in Natural Systems.* Washington, DC: World Wildlife Fund, 2003.

Huber, Walter L. "The John Muir Trail." *Sierra Club Bulletin* 15 (1930): 37–46.

Jensen, Mari N. "More Large Forest Fires Linked to Climate Change." News release posted by University of Arizona Laboratory of Tree-Ring Research at *University of Arizona News,* uanews.org, July 6, 2006.

Keller, Robert H., and Michael F. Turek. *American Indians and National Parks.* Tucson: University of Arizona Press, 1998.

Le Conte, Joseph N. "Among the Sources of the South Fork of the King's River—Part I." *Sierra Club Bulletin* 4 (1903): 177–184.

———. "Among the Sources of the South Fork of the King's River—Part II." *Sierra Club Bulletin* 4 (1903): 253–263.

Leopold, Aldo. *Round River.* Oxford: Oxford University Press, 1993.

Leopold, A. Starker, et al. "Wildlife Management in the National Parks." In *Transactions of the Twenty-eighth North American Wildlife and Natural Resources Conference.* Washington, DC: Wildlife Management Institute, 1963. Reprinted in Lary M. Dilsaver, *America's National Park System: The Critical Documents* (Lanham, MD: Rowman and Littlefield, 1994).

Louter, David. *Windshield Wilderness: Cars, Roads, and Nature in Washington's National Parks.* Seattle: University of Washington Press, 2006.

Louv, Richard. *Last Child in the Woods: Saving Our Children from Nature-Deficit Disorder.* Chapel Hill, NC: Algonquin Books, 2005.

Mann, Charles C. *1491: New Revelations of the Americas before Columbus.* New York: Alfred A. Knopf, 2005.

McClelland, Linda Flint. *Building the National Parks: Historic Landscape Design and Construction.* Baltimore: Johns Hopkins University Press, 1998.

Muir, John. *The Mountains of California.* New York: Century Company, 1894.

———. *My First Summer in the Sierra.* New York: Houghton Mifflin, 1911.

———. *Our National Parks.* New York: Houghton Mifflin, 1901.

National Academy of Sciences, National Research Council. *A Report by the Advisory Committee to the National Park Service on Research.* August 1, 1963. Reprinted in Lary M. Dilsaver, *America's National Park System: The Critical Documents* (Lanham, MD: Rowman and Littlefield, 1994).

Pergams, Oliver R. W., and Patricia A. Zaradic. "Evidence for a Fundamental and Pervasive Shift away from Nature-Based Recreation." *PNAS* 105 (2007): 2295–2300.

Randall, Ralph. *Report to the Federal Power Commission on the Storage Resources of the South and Middle Forks of the Kings River, California.* Washington, DC: Federal Power Commission, 1930.

Roth, Hal. *Pathway in the Sky: The Story of the John Muir Trail.* Berkeley, CA: Howell North Books, 1965.

Sargent, Shirley. *Solomons of the Sierra: The Pioneer of the John Muir Trail.* Yosemite, CA: Flying Spur Press, 1989.

Sellars, Richard West. *Preserving Nature in the National Parks: A History.* New Haven, CT: Yale University Press, 1997.

Shankland, Robert. *Steve Mather of the National Parks.* New York: Alfred A. Knopf, 1951.

Snyder, Gary. *The Practice of the Wild.* New York: North Point Press, 1990.

Solomons, Theodore. "Beginnings of the John Muir Trail." *Sierra Club Bulletin* 25 (1940): 28–40.

Spence, Mark David. *Dispossessing the Wilderness: Indian Removal and the Making of the National Parks.* Oxford: Oxford University Press, 1999.

United States Department of Defense. *R-2508 Complex User's Handbook.* 2009. Available at www.edwards.af.mil/shared/media/document/AFD-070103-052.pdf.

United States Department of the Interior, National Park Service. *Management Policies 2006.* Washington, DC: U.S. Department of the Interior, 2006.

United States Forest Service. *The Use of the National Forests.* Washington, DC: Department of Agriculture, 1907.

United States Government Accountability Office. *Climate Change: Agencies Should Develop Guidance for Addressing the Effect on Federal Lands and Water Resources.* GAO-07-863. Washington, DC: Government Accountability Office, 2007.

Van Mantgem, P.J., and N.L. Stephenson. "Apparent Climatically Induced Increase of Tree Mortality Rates in a Temperate Forest." *Ecology Letter* 10 (2007): 909–916.

White, Stewart Edward. *Camp and Trail.* New York: Outing Company, 1907.

Winks, Robin. "Robin Winks on the Evolution and Meaning of the Organic Act." *George Wright Forum* 24 (2007): 7–21.

Worster, Donald. *A Passion for Nature: The Life of John Muir.* Oxford: Oxford University Press, 2008.

———. *The Wealth of Nature: Environmental History and the Ecological Imagination.* Oxford: Oxford University Press, 1994.

ACKNOWLEDGMENTS

Inspiration for this book came from thousands of anonymous visitors to Sequoia and Kings Canyon National Parks. In ways that I cannot overestimate, their persistent questions made me think. Without their quiet input, this book would not exist.

Although the conclusions in this book are mine, and mine alone, dozens of perceptive minds have supplied useful suggestions and direction.

Within the National Park Service, many provided ideas or active encouragement, including, at Sequoia and Kings Canyon, superintendent Craig Axtell and wilderness coordinator Gregg Fauth. Dr. David Graber, Pacific West regional scientist for the agency, provided much useful feedback, as did John Reynolds, now retired from the agency but at various times a regional director and the agency's deputy director in Washington, D.C. And special thanks go to NPS director Jonathan B. Jarvis, who not only provided a foreword to this book but also, and far more importantly, continues to serve as a real leader in the effort to protect our parks and all their resources.

222 / Acknowledgments

Thank you to NPS wilderness rangers George Durkee, Dave Gordon, Dario Malengo, Allison Stein, and Nina Weisman for the insights into wilderness issues that they shared with me both during my hike and at other times. Several of these dedicated employees also assisted me with the placement of food caches.

Dr. Nate Stephenson, a research ecologist with the United States Geological Survey, was especially generous with both his time and his thoughts, and I am deeply appreciative of his efforts and support.

Steven Trimble, David Louter of the National Park Service, and Dr. Louis Warren of the University of California, Davis, each read the manuscript at critical moments and offered useful and perceptive comments. Their efforts improved the book significantly, as did the suggestions provided by Peter Stekel.

During my first year of work on this book, Gary Snyder sat with me for a day in the wilderness of Sequoia National Park and shared ideas that I hope I have done justice to. In his ninth decade, Gary remains an inspiration to many who hike the Sierra's trails.

Phyllis Faber provided encouragement at critical moments and helped advance the project in many ways.

Thanks go to Lloyd Holland and his family at Lost Valley Ranch for their hospitality. I owe similar thanks to Carolyn Pistilli, long-time manager extraordinaire of the Bearpaw Meadow High Sierra Camp.

At the University of California Press, Jenny Wapner encouraged me in a thousand ways. Lynn Meinhardt answered a thousand questions and solved countless minor problems. Jacqueline Volin and Bonita Hurd shepherded me through the editing and production processes, and their patient efforts improved the book in many ways.

Mark Williams of Eureka Cartography in Berkeley, California, drafted this volume's maps. Special thanks go to Matthew Rangel, who generously allowed me to use as illustrations for this book portions of his lithographic exhibit *a transect—due east*. In his work, Matthew does a wonderful job of capturing what makes the Sierra so special to so many of us.

Malinee Crapsey provided invaluable assistance during the proofreading process.

To my old friend Armando Quintero, who shared with me not only much of the hike recorded in this book but also valuable thoughts on many national-park-related ideas, I owe thanks for two decades of wilderness companionship.

And finally, I owe unique thanks to my wife, Frances, whose support made possible not only this book but also so many other wonderful things.

INDEX

Italicized page references indicate illustrations.

234 / *Index*

Text: 10/15 Janson
Display: Janson
Indexer: Marcia Carlson
Compositor: BookMatters, Berkeley